Jews:
Nearly Everything You Wanted to Know*

*but were too afraid to ask

Jews: Nearly Everything You Wanted to Know*
*but were too afraid to ask

Wonderfully entertaining, eminently readable, and mind-blowingly informative! A book of beguiling subtleties that demonstrates the authors' comprehensive and authoritative knowledge of their subject.

*Martin O'Kane, Professor of Biblical Studies
University of Wales Trinity St David*

A lively and light approach to some very protracted issues – it is a thoughtful introduction to a complex issue, nicely broken down into some of the most central arguments.

Oliver Leaman, Professor of Philosophy and Zantker Professor of Judaic Studies University of Kentucky

Take two smart fellows in philosophy and theology, give them a seemingly simple question – 'What is a Jew?' – then sit back and watch them spin web upon web of complexity. It is to laugh. Not to mention, to learn a great deal.

Daniel Klein, American best-selling author

Any book which poses difficult questions on Jews and Judaism is bound to be controversial. This challenging debate between a rabbi and a philosopher, including some intriguing role reversals, does not disappoint.

*Rabbi Professor Jonathan Magonet,
formerly Principal of Leo Baeck College, London*

We can all learn more about Judaism and there is nowhere better than here – serious subjects, accompanied by a light touch, sensitive disagreement and (crucial to Judaism) Jewish jokes.

*The Very Rev Christopher Lewis,
formerly Dean of Christ Church, Oxford*

Jews:
Nearly Everything You Wanted to Know*

*but were too afraid to ask

Peter Cave
and Dan Cohn-Sherbok

with illustrations by Dan Cohn-Sherbok

SHEFFIELD UK   BRISTOL CT

Published by Equinox Publishing Ltd.

UK: Office 415, The Workstation, 15 Paternoster Row, Sheffield, South Yorkshire S1 2BX
USA: ISD, 70 Enterprise Drive, Bristol, CT 06010

www.equinoxpub.com

First published 2018

© Peter Cave and Dan Cohn-Sherbok 2018

All rights reserved. No part of this publication may be reproduced or transmitted in any form or by any means, electronic or mechanical, including photocopying, recording or any information storage or retrieval system, without prior permission in writing from the publishers.

British Library Cataloguing-in-Publication Data

A catalogue record for this book is available from the British Library.

ISBN-13   978 1 78179 777 8   (paperback)
          978 1 78179 778 5   (ePDF)

Library of Congress Cataloguing-in-Publication Data

Names: Cave, Peter, author. | Cohn-Sherbok, Dan, author.
Title: Jews: Nearly Everything You Wanted to Know* *but were too afraid to ask / Peter Cave and Dan Cohn-Sherbok.
Description: Sheffield, UK; Bristol, CT: Equinox Publishing Ltd, 2018. | Includes bibliographical references and index.
Identifiers: LCCN 2018012271 (print) | LCCN 2018012733 (ebook) | ISBN 9781781797785 (ePDF) | ISBN 9781781797778 (pb)
Subjects: LCSH: Jews—Identity. | Judaism. | Israel.
Classification: LCC DS143 (ebook) | LCC DS143 .C38 2018 (print) | DDC 956.94—dc23
LC record available at https://lccn.loc.gov/2018012271

Typeset by S.J.I. Services, New Delhi, India
Printed and bound by Lightning Source Inc. (La Vergne, TN), Lightning Source UK Ltd. (Milton Keynes), Lightning Source AU Pty. (Scoresby, Victoria).

Dedicated (courtesy of Maimonides) to:

those who are perplexed – and those who are not

About the authors

Peter Cave read philosophy at University College London and King's College Cambridge. His philosophy lectureships span University College London, University of Khartoum, Sudan, to, currently, the Open University and New York University (London).

Peter is a Fellow of the Royal Society of Arts and until recently served as a member of the Council of the Royal Institute of Philosophy. He is Patron of Humanists UK and Population Matters. He has published numerous papers, light and serious. His books include *This Sentence is False: an introduction to philosophical paradoxes* and three 'beginner's guides': *Humanism*; *Philosophy*; and *Ethics*. His most recent work is *The Big Think Book: Discover Philosophy Through 99 Perplexing Puzzles*. He has written and presented philosophy programmes for BBC radio, and often takes part in public debates on ethics, religion and socio-political matters, as well as philosophy, of course.

Peter lives in Soho in central London, enjoys opera, lieder and chamber music (well, he thinks he knows what he likes), and, despite his atheism, even delights in religious music. He is irritated by builders' drillings, pointless burglar alarms and unnecessary thuds of music in cafés, restaurants and shops. He is often to be found with a glass of wine – or two.

Dan Cohn-Sherbok is an American rabbi and Professor Emeritus of Judaism at the University of Wales. He received a PhD from the University of Cambridge and an Honorary Doctorate of Divinity from the Hebrew Union College-Jewish Institute of Religion, New York.

Dan is the author and editor of many books dealing with Judaism and Israel including *Israel: The History of an Idea*; *The Palestine-Israeli Conflict* (with Dawoud El-Alami); *Debating Israel and Palestine* (with Mary Grey); *The Politics of Apocalypse: The History and Influence of Christian Zionism*; *Introduction to Zionism and Israel: From Ideology to History*; and *The Palestinian State: A Jewish Justification*. He has published several books of cartoons.

Dan lives in Kensington in London as well as in Wales with his wife Lavinia and his Burmese cat. He is frequently to be found drawing cartoons in his London club.

Contents

Prologue		xi
Part One: Jews, Judaism and Jerusalem		**1**
1	Who is a Jew?	3
2	What is Judaism?	17
3	What is Jewish morality?	29
4	Do Jews not care about animal welfare?	42
5	Zionism: 'Next year, in Jerusalem' – but whose Jerusalem?	55
6	Does the Holocaust make Israel's existence a special case?	69
7	Why are Jews so hated?	82
Part Two: Israel: 'This land is our land'		**95**
8	Is there a future for Jews and Judaism outside of Israel?	97
9	What determines a nation's territorial rights?	110
10	Are Jews collectively responsible for Israeli military actions?	124

11	One state, two states or no-state-at-all solution – and where?	137
12	Are not Muslims better off in Israel than in Islamic states?	150
13	Does Israel deserve to lose the sympathy vote to the Palestinians?	164
14	Boycotts: should we stop buying Israel's avocados, dates and pomegranates?	177

Part Three: Israel, integrity and reasons to wail — **191**

15	Can Israel be a Jewish state – and if so, for how long?	193
16	Can a Jewish state be a liberal democracy, avoiding apartheid?	206
17	'Scratch an anti-Zionist and you'll find an antisemite.' Really?	219
18	Are anti-Zionist Jews nothing but self-hating Jews?	233
19	Does Jewish humour show Jews to be unfit for a state of their own?	245
20	What has Israel done for the Jews?	257
21	What has Israel done for the world?	270
Epilogue		284
Bibliography		294
Further reading		296
Index		299

Prologue

The authors have known each other for some years; they occasionally have tea together at their London Pall Mall club. The location is far removed from the horrendous sufferings and struggles in the outside world, but Dan, with his rabbinical hat, and Peter, with his philosophical despair over ethical dilemmas, would often reflect on 'what can be done', though neither were in much of a position to do much at all. Hereafter, we speak with separate voices.

Peter Cave sees the venture thus:

'What a mess! What chaos!' I was expressing despairing thoughts when speaking to my yet-to-be co-author, Dan. My references were to Israel's bombing of Palestinian sites, causing considerable suffering and death, and to some Palestinians, often courtesy of Hamas's thinking, firing numerous rockets at Israel, sometimes with deathly results.

Dan apart, my Jewish friends – atheists indeed, often philosophers – typically have knee-jerk reactions in favour of Israeli military attacks on Palestinians; they perceive anti-Israeli remarks as heading towards antisemitism, Judeophobia or Jew-hatred (we use those expressions interchangeably). My non-Jewish friends typically have knee-jerk reactions against the Israeli attacks and find ridiculous the idea that criticisms of Israel, even justified criticisms of Israel's military actions, are thereby antisemitic.

I typically sit somewhere in the middle, astonished that one side fails to grasp the viewpoint of the other. Further, there seems little room for rational debate in public. Even debate concerning whether criticism of Israeli policies counts as antisemitism may, these days, be viewed as antisemitic; and that is so, notwithstanding the fact that some critics are manifestly Jewish and prepared to challenge the mainstream Jewish establishment.

Regarding both Israeli/Palestinian conflicts and antisemitic charges, I was intrigued that Dan, rabbi and Professor of Judaism, was prepared to engage in discussion, without knee-jerks. Mind you, I realized that Dan was of the "Reform model" of the rabbinic, so probably as wishy-washy as I can be.

Thus, it was from the 'What a mess!' that this book developed. I also had slight personal interest. I was brought up lowly, by loving parents, as Baptist, ignorant of Jewry. Throughout my adult life, courtesy of my appearance, bleak quips and guilt wailings, most acquaintances assume me Jewish. After my mother's death, slight evidence hinted at that assumption's truth, cohering with the shame that once accompanied illegitimate births – an ethos that blighted many lives. Who knows?

Dan and I value humour in life; and Dan has the talent to draw and recall numerous Jewish jokes. Therefore, we felt it appropriate to include some relevant examples and 'oy vey's. Let us remember:

> A lightness of touch need not imply that what is touched is not deep – deeply serious, deeply perplexing, deeply important.

Dan Cohn-Sherbok says more, regarding 'why this book?'

Israel is constantly in the news, with the Palestinian protests in Gaza against the establishment of a US embassy in Jerusalem in May 2018 making recent international headlines. It was not surprising, therefore, that Israeli policy was the topic of our conversation. Our talk ranged from Jewish attitudes toward the Palestinians to the general subject of antisemitism and what it means to be Jewish in the modern world. Peter was particularly concerned with recent allegations against British Labour politicians as being antisemitic.

Over the last few decades, numerous books have been published dealing with modern Jewish history, the emergence of the Jewish state, the Middle East conflict, the plight of Palestinians, the history of antisemitism, and a variety of related subjects. I have myself published several books dealing with these topics, as well as general introductions to Judaism. Yet, only infrequently do authors engage in debate about issues related to what it means to be Jewish in contemporary society and the creation of Israel and its relationship to the Jewish heritage. It is rare that such subjects are dealt with from a philosophical perspective as we did that afternoon.

There is thus a need for open debate and dialogue concerning fundamental questions about Jewishness, antisemitism, the creation of a Jewish state, its connection with Jewish values, and its role in the life of contemporary Jewry. As an atheist, humanistic philosopher, Peter is well-equipped to deal with a wide range of intriguing and perplexing questions.

Throughout this volume, I, in my own voice, have sought in each chapter to set the stage for discussion, and readers will readily see that our approaches are strikingly different. We have also attempted to enliven our otherwise serious debate by including some relevant Jewish jokes, illustrated with my cartoons. Jewish humour, often self-deprecating, is an essential part of Jewish life, and its inclusion gives a flavour of what it means to be Jewish. Each of us has posed questions for readers at the end of every chapter.

The book itself is divided into three parts. The first opens up the discussion by raising questions regarding Jewish identity, morality, and the cause of antisemitism. As the term 'semite' refers to both Jews and Arabs, rather than writing 'anti-Semitism', we write 'antisemitism' to mean hostility to, prejudice, or discrimination specifically against Jews. Part Two concentrates on topics related to Israel itself, exploring a nation's territorial rights, collective responsibility, the Palestinians and so forth. Finally, in Part Three, we focus on the nature of a Jewish state, anti-Zionism, Jewish humour and the meaning of Israel for contemporary Jewry. The book concludes with reflections by both of us.

It is our hope that this debate will stimulate others to ponder critical questions regarding Judaism generally and more particularly the Jewish state, its significance for modern Jews and non-Jews, and its role in world affairs – and, to use Peter's expression, without 'knee-jerk' reactions.

Part One
Jews, Judaism and Jerusalem

Chapter One
Who is a Jew?

1.1 DAN starts us off:

You might think the answer to the question 'Who is a Jew?' is simple. But it isn't. Jews have been around for thousands of years, but there is considerable uncertainty about who is a Jew. Whenever I try to explain the complexities of Jewish identity to my students, I take a toy rabbit to class. I hold it up by its ears. And I ask: 'What is this?' They say: 'A rabbit.' And I then ask them to list the criteria for this toy being a rabbit and not something else. The list includes: big ears, four paws, whiskers, and so on.

And then I draw a cartoon of a woman on the whiteboard. And I say: 'This is a Jewish woman.' But there isn't anything that one can point to in the same way that identifies this person as Jewish. It is a matter of definition. In other words, Jewishness isn't anything empirical. It is an identity that is dependent on the Jewish community's understanding of who is a Jew and who is not.

So, if you ask 'who is a Jew?', there is no single answer. Instead there are complex, conflicting views which divide the Jewish community. It is commonly said that if you have three Jews, there are five different opinions.

1.2 PETER muses – with some bafflement:

Reading Dan's introduction, I pictured a definitional rabbit conjured from a moth-eaten Hasidic shtreimel (fur hat). Happily, no rabbit – well, no clean-living rabbit – appeared. Dan's opening remarks, if I may be so bold, baffle me; after all, to tell whether something is a rabbit, and not a toy, we need to check innards. Dan, please consider: 'What is art?'

When we see in art galleries not just works by Rubens, Rembrandt and Raphael, or even those of Matisse, Munch and Modigliani, but Malevich's *Black Square*, the odd urinal and a dishevelled bed courtesy of Ms. Tracey Emin, we wonder: what is art? With such motley collections, art, some suggest, is whatever art curators, such as those in New York, consider as art. That is futile; it engages a circular definition. How are art curators recognized as such? How do they know what to consider?

Who is a Jew? Dan answers, 'Jewishness depends on the Jewish community's understanding of who is a Jew'. We are cast into definitional circular seas, now with waves of doubled trouble. How do we spot the Jewish community? How does that community judge who is a Jew?

We first learn words not by dictionary definitions, but by exposure to wordy applications. 'Meaning is use' is the slogan, derived from the highly influential twentieth-century Jewish philosopher Ludwig Wittgenstein. By the way, Dan, a few – well, Kimberley Cornish – speculate that Wittgenstein as clever, arrogant schoolboy contributed to Hitler's antisemitism, for Hitler overlapped with him when at Linz's *Realschule*.

Returning to definitions, few of us know definitions of horses, homes and happiness; yet most of us can tell when we meet with a horse, feel bad at avoiding eye contact with the homeless, and possess yearnings for happiness. That does not mean that we never err. It does not mean that there are no grey areas.

How do we recognize Jews? We do so by a variety of external features, none of which is essential for Jewishness, none of which is sufficient. There are certain attitudes, rituals and dress; various physical traits, humours and names. There may be smatterings of Hebrew, some Yiddish terms and klezmer keenness. Yarmulkes (skullcaps), menorahs (seven-armed lamps) and wigs may be on view; the Torah read; significance given to feasts such as the Passover. Perhaps there is a mezuzah – a handwritten scroll, I gather, of the Shema prayer within a case usually fixed to the home's doorpost. Occasional synagogue attendances and bar/bat mitzvah ceremonies could be noted – and, more intimately so, male circumcisions. There may well be manifestations of a sense of continuity and identification with a people – the Jews, the Israelites – as recorded in the Hebrew Bible, stretching forward through the centuries to the recent horrendous sufferings in the Holocaust.

Deploying a Wittgensteinian concept, 'Jew' is a family resemblance term, one which draws on cultural, physical and religious features. There are similarities and dissimilarities between Jews – just as there are between members of the same family. That, I suspect, may lead you, Dan, into the role of Jewish ancestry.

1.3 DAN sees a conundrum:

I have only touched on the problem of Jewishness. There simply isn't a single definition. The Hebrew Bible doesn't lay down any precise definition of Jewishness. But in ancient times it was assumed that if a person has a Jewish father, then that person is Jewish. As time passed, the rabbis redefined Jewishness as dependent on maternal descent. However, it has always been possible to join the Jewish people through conversion. Orthodox Judaism lays down strict rules about conversion and refuses to accept converts who have converted to Judaism from other Jewish movements. These non-Orthodox movements, however, accept Orthodox converts as Jews.

> **Are you Jewish?**
>
> A woman on a train walks up to a man in the dining car. 'Excuse me,' she says, 'but are you Jewish?'
>
> 'No,' he replies.
>
> A few minutes later the woman returns. 'Sorry to bother you again,' she says, 'Sure you're not Jewish?'
>
> 'I'm sure,' insists the man.
>
> A few minutes later she goes up to the man a third time and quizzes, 'Are you absolutely sure you're not Jewish?'
>
> 'All right, all right,' he sighs, 'You win. I am Jewish.'
>
> 'Funny,' says the woman, 'You don't look Jewish.'

Matters become more confusing by the recent decision of the Reform movement to accept as Jews individuals whose fathers are Jewish but whose mothers are non-Jews. Within Reform Judaism, both matrilineal and patrilineal descent are viewed as sufficient criteria for being Jewish: if either your father or mother is Jewish, then you are Jewish. The Orthodox, however, will not accept as Jews those whose father is Jewish but whose mother is not. In such cases, the person is regarded as a non-Jew. There is further confusion regarding Messianic Jews – even if they were born of Jewish matrilineal descent, they are regarded by the general Jewish community as outsiders because they believe in Jesus. There is thus no universal agreement within the Jewish world about the definition of who is a Jew.

You drew an analogy with art. But that is fundamentally different from the thorny issues surrounding the question 'Who is a Jew?'. This is not a philosophical dilemma. It is a conundrum about the definition of Jewry, not about 'family resemblances'. The Orthodox and the non-Orthodox have different criteria of Jewishness. They have adopted different procedures of conversion. There is a fundamental disagreement about the status of patrilineal descent. In addition, Orthodox and non-Orthodox Jews continually wage war against each other about requirements of membership within the community.

I once considered joining an Orthodox synagogue close to my London home. I am a Reform rabbi. But for the Orthodox, that is not good enough. I had to demonstrate my maternal Jewish descent. If my parents had a marriage certificate from an Orthodox synagogue, that would be sufficient because the Orthodox marry only Jews. But my parents were married in a Reform synagogue. However, my mother's mother was buried in an Orthodox cemetery. So, since the Orthodox bury only Jews, her burial certificate would be sufficient to demonstrate my Jewishness to the Orthodox. That's an example of the complexity.

As for rabbits, they are not, contrary to what you imply, in the same boat as Jews. We all know what a rabbit is through observation. No matter what word is used to refer to one, a rabbit is a rabbit. We do not need a definition. But given the complexities of determining Jewishness, definitions and criteria are indispensable. Without them, there is utter confusion.

1.4 PETER challenges further:

You tell me, Dan, that a rabbit is a rabbit; that is as uninformative as my surmising that a Jew is a Jew. Of course, whether someone is a Jew is far more important than whether a creature is a rabbit – except to rabbits – and far more important than whether items exhibited in New York's Museum of Modern Art are works of art.

You appear to be seeking an elusive essence of Jewry, a set of features that all Jews must have in common, making them Jews. I give you water.

For centuries, water was basically understood as a liquid that is colourless, tasteless, odourless and which quenches thirst. Scientists now say, having investigated microstructures, that if you want to be water, you had better be mainly H_2O. Their classification of water as H_2O is, they hope, 'carving nature at its joints', identifying a real grouping within nature, distinct from, say, wine.

Where does this leave the Jews? 'In a muddle.' There are competing authorities; some seek to carve at divinely created joints, perhaps to separate the chosen people, 'the Jews', from others. If you believe in that divine intent – or value it as metaphor – then it is highly important that you get the carving right. Do we, though, seriously think that there is a right way of carving here?

I see no good reason to suppose an essence that grounds the identity of Jews. We have no problem, in the main, in recognizing typical Orthodox and non-Orthodox Jews, Hasidic and Reform – and, for that matter, atheistic Jews. There is no need to assume or to establish matrilineal or patrilineal descent – the historical genetic microstructure, so to speak – to find Jews.

How would or should Jewish communities respond were it now discovered that ancestors of some – perhaps their most eminent rabbis – lacked correct lineage? Must they be exiled? Should they at least be safe from antisemitism? Similar questions arise regarding a family who have been thoroughly imbued in the Chinese community for generations, without a hint of current Jewishness, yet which turns out to have appropriate Jewish lineage. Must they hence be treated as Jewish? That would surely be crazy.

1.5 DAN wrestles on:

You are right, Peter, that the question 'Who is a Jew?' is a muddle. Jews themselves cannot make up their mind. It depends whom you ask. You would think that, after thousands of years, Jews would know who belongs to the Jewish tribe. But they don't. As you say, some Jews – particularly Orthodox – seek divine authority for their views. Some Orthodox Jewish thinkers once argued that that there is such a thing as a Jewish soul, different from gentile souls. Yet, even though this is no longer a widely shared view, the Orthodox still believe that the criteria they apply to determine who is Jewish are of divine origin.

You suggest there are family resemblances among Jews consisting of similarities of appearance, interests, rituals, activities, dress and values. It is on this basis, you assert, that Jews can be recognized. But I do not think this actually applies to Jews. Recently, my wife and I sat in a Tel Aviv café, watching Jews pass by. Their diversity was astonishing. There were black Jews from Ethiopia, Orthodox Jews wearing yarmulkes, blonde women in very skimpy clothes, businessmen wearing suits, dark-skinned children on bicycles, Oriental Jews in jeans. No doubt their religious views were as diverse as their appearance. What was missing was any sense of the family resemblances you suggested.

In the Jewish community, identifying Jews is not by family resemblances. Instead, as I stressed, Jews appeal to specific criteria of Jewishness. The problem is that they cannot agree on the criteria.

What, then, is my response to the question 'Who is a Jew?' I am aware of the variety of answers across the Jewish spectrum. Everyone thinks they know. But do they really? As I have been suggesting, Jewishness is an elusive concept. There really is no such thing – just a range of conventional definitions at odds with each other. I have been a rabbi on four continents, ministering to Jews from Alabama to Australia, from London to Johannesburg, from Illinois to Colorado. Who is a Jew? Who knows? Not me.

1.6 PETER, with the last word(s):

Dan, you hanker after a defining essence of Jewishness, find it elusive – and conclude, with sadness, that there is none, though you sound as if you still hope to find one. You are right in your conclusion, but foolish in the hope. Unlike circles and squares where there are essences, Jews are a variety of flesh-and-blood people.

Try Wittgenstein on 'games'. We recognize games, yet they radically differ: football, patience, chess, Monopoly, playing 'chase', the Olympics, Tetris, the erotic, guessing, 'rock, paper, scissors' and so on. True, they are all called 'games', but there is no one thread, no essence, that justifies use of the term for them all; yet the term is not ambiguous. Contrast with 'bank' by a river and 'bank' as a financial institution, where there is ambiguity.

Now, Dan, you observed an astonishing array of Jews: black Ethiopian, yarmulke-clad, blondes in skimpy clothes, and so forth. Curiously, you managed to pick them all out as Jews. Was that by magic? By rabbinical intuition? Of course not. You told by appearances, though occasionally you may have erred. A common way of telling is that the individuals concerned accept the accolade 'Jewish'. They may own up, on the basis of having Jewish parents; that is, they pass the meaning buck of 'Jew' to earlier generations, when, for Jewish identification, as now, there was reliance on dress, commitments, appearances *et al* – and maybe more buck passing.

In Lewis Carroll's *Through the Looking Glass*, Alice is baffled by Humpty Dumpty's comment 'There's glory for you'. HD explains that by 'glory' he means 'a nice knock-down argument'. Alice protests: 'glory' does not mean 'a nice knock-down argument'. HD replies, 'When I use a word, it means just what I choose it to mean.' HD sought to be master of his meanings, yet things are not that easy; we are enmeshed within a common language.

Recognizing that typically we cannot just make up meanings, many Jews may insist that there must be 'the' right meaning of 'Jew', an essence of Jewishness, set by reality, perhaps by God, behind the mish-mash of appearances. Whatever, though, is that essence? If it comes down to lineage, then we have the bizarre discoveries mentioned in my previous response – of some rabbis no longer being Jews and a Chinese family now being deemed Jewish.

Your evaluation of Jewishness as 'elusive' betrays a yearning for something yet to be discovered, Dan. Or is it a scent that lingers from your Jewish nurturing and rabbinical trainings? Perhaps things will become clearer when you lead us not, I trust, into temptation, but into the nature of Judaism.

> **Mullings**
>
> Dan asks:
> Does it make sense to think that a fervent atheist could ever be an authentic Jew?
>
> Peter asks:
> Who is master of the term 'Jew'? Orthodox Jew? Reform Jew? Atheist Jew? Non-Jew? Antisemite?

Chapter Two
What is Judaism?

2.1 DAN writes:

If you look at most introductory textbooks about Judaism, the impression frequently given is that Judaism is a uniform religious tradition. But this is entirely misleading. Throughout history there have been many kinds of Judaism. In ancient times, biblical Judaism centred around the Temple. However, with the destruction of the Temple by the Romans in the first century, a new kind of Judaism – Rabbinic Judaism – took the place of biblical Judaism.

In the modern period, the Jewish religion has further fragmented into a wide range of 'Judaisms' which are radically different from one another. On the far right of the spectrum is Hasidism. Alongside the Hasidim, strictly Orthodox Jews adhere to the *Shulhan Arukh* (the Code of Jewish Law). Moving along the spectrum, a variety of non-Orthodox movements emerged. At the beginning of the nineteenth century, Reform Judaism

> **Synagogues: one, two, three**
>
> Cohen and Goldberg were stranded on a desert island. They worked together, creating a store, workshop, villa – and three synagogues. One day there is a shipwreck, and a passenger, Christina Jones, manages to reach the island. She is met by Cohen and Goldberg who take her on a tour of their island. They come across two of the synagogues.
>
> 'Why two?' asks Ms. Jones, innocent of Jewish ways.
>
> 'Well,' explains Cohen, 'I wouldn't be seen dead in Goldberg's – and Goldberg feels the same about mine.'
>
> Ms. Jones then sees the third synagogue. 'But why a third?' she asks.
>
> 'Ah, that's the one neither of us would be seen dead in,' Cohen and Goldberg reply in unison.

called for the reformulation of Judaism to meet the needs of the contemporary world. Subsequently, Conservative Judaism similarly rejected the authority of Orthodox rabbis, but adopted a more conservative approach to Jewish law.

In the early twentieth century, Reconstructionist Judaism – a non-theistic movement – developed as an outgrowth of Conservative Judaism. Later, Humanistic Judaism similarly abandoned a belief in a supernatural deity and adopted an even more radical approach to the Jewish tradition.

This brief survey of the Jewish past illustrates that, paradoxically, there is no single Jewish 'Judaism'.

2.2 PETER reflects:

Well, Dan, with such a variety of Judaisms – a Heinz fifty-seven variety? – do not Jews wonder why they should have belief in any of them?

The 'Why believe?' question has three readings. We may ask, first, what caused the belief to arise; secondly, why the belief should be accepted as true; and thirdly, whether the belief is held with some aim in mind.

Let us try an analogy: Larry believes that Ludmilla is passionately in love with him. How should we account for his belief?

Here is a causal explanation: Larry's friends injected his brain, generating his 'love' belief or perhaps they hypnotized him into the belief. The causal explanation does not justify Larry's belief as true; it is but an explanation of the fact that the belief arose. A bang on the head could have causally accounted for the belief.

Whatever the causes, we may wonder whether there is good reason or justification – good evidence – for Larry's belief being true. Perhaps there is: maybe he overheard Ludmilla saying how much she loved him; maybe she has expressed that love in the ways of erotica. Of course, Larry may unwittingly have bad reasons for his belief; Ludmilla could have been feigning her romantic devotion, with her eyes on Larry's bank balance.

The third question is: what is Larry's aim in having such a belief? That may lead us to wonder about his psychological state. Larry says, 'I cannot live without Ludmilla; I couldn't bear to think of her not loving me.' That may express no authentic belief, but more a desperate hope, even an obsession – one that helps Larry get through life.

Return to Judaism, be it any of the fifty-seven flavours or the 'one true flavour'. No doubt, there are causal explanations for any current Judaic belief – for any belief at all. Further, the Judaic beliefs may help believers to get through life, embraced by the Jewish community. My question is: whatever good justification – reasons, evidence – can be given for those Judaic beliefs at Judaism's heart being true?

2.3 DAN engages the challenge:

You ask: why believe in Judaism? But what beliefs are you referring to? Orthodox? Reform? Conservative? Reconstructionist? Humanistic? The belief systems are profoundly different. There is no single form of Judaism. Let me begin with the Orthodox. According to Orthodoxy, these are the fundamental Jewish beliefs:

1. God's existence
2. God's unity
3. God's incorporeality
4. God's eternity
5. God alone is to be worshipped
6. Belief in prophecy
7. Moses was the greatest of the prophets
8. God revealed the Torah to Moses
9. The Torah is unchangeable
10. God's omniscience
11. Reward and punishment
12. The Messiah
13. Resurrection of the dead

Through centuries, strictly Orthodox Jews have subscribed to those key ideas and principles. But today's non-Orthodox Jews reject many of the beliefs because they seem completely implausible. Most modern non-Orthodox Jews have subjected the tradition to rational consideration, and they accept only those elements of Jewish heritage which appear plausible, sensible and coherent.

Consequently, in the Jewish community there are profound disagreements over what constitutes 'true' Judaism. Don't forget that there are even non-theistic branches (Reconstructionist and Humanistic Judaism) which reject any idea of a supernatural deity. But despite such conflict, there is a general recognition that belief is not the key reason for why a person is Jewish. Jewishness is not essentially a matter of belief. You treat the subject as though it is a philosophical issue. Being Jewish is essentially a question of ethnic identity.

2.4 PETER battles on:

In my innocence, I was under the impression that here we are discussing Judaism – the religion – rather than continuing with Jewish identity. For the avoidance of doubt, as my legal friends say, I assume that Judaism is distinct from Jewishness. Many people are Jewish (under some of Chapter One's criteria) yet have no belief in any form of Judaism and, for that matter, have no engagement with the synagogue. Further, I assume that it is possible – though maybe rare – that someone be a believer in a version of Judaism, yet not be accepted as Jewish by ethnicity. Being Jewish is neither necessary nor sufficient for commitment to Judaism.

Whichever version of Judaism is in the frame, we should ask for the grounds – reasons, justification – for holding its distinctive beliefs as true. Without those, the beliefs need either to be blindingly self-evident or, in some way, matters of faith. That latter option introduces the Protestant Danish philosopher, Søren Kierkegaard. Kierkegaard argued that religious believers take 'leaps of faith' – I call him a 'kangaroo' believer. Curiously, there are no hops, skips or jumps.

Judaic leaps are stimulated, I assume, by the Hebrew Bible, Jewish traditions and synagogue activities. Of course, those stimulants may lead some Jews into rejecting Judaism as a phantasy. Phantasies can be fun – though sometimes disturbing.

Jews love to argue, as do philosophers. On what grounds do believers in different versions of Judaism argue? To put it picturesquely, how do they justify their different leaps of faith and over which abyss – some leaping into, for example, ultra-Orthodoxy of Hasidism, some into mainstream Orthodoxy, some into Reform? How do they, more generally, seek to justify their commitment to Judaism as the true religion rather

> **Jews: committed to Judaism?**
>
> A young Jewish boy goes off to college and is told by his father to date only Jewish girls, lest he fall in love with and marry a shiksa, a girl who is not Jewish. The boy, though, does fall in love – and she is gentile. To his father's chagrin, he marries her and she converts to Judaism. In fact, she quickly becomes a devout, practising Jew. They have children.
>
> The father calls his son one day, informs him he has purchased a new boat, and invites the son and family for what promises to be a wonderful day of sailing. The son reminds his father that it is Shabbos and his wife, being highly observant, will not be able to join them.
>
> 'See, I told you to marry a Jewish girl!' groans the father.

than that of Islam, Satanism or Christianity with its Trinity of God, the Son and the Holy Ghost?

2.5 DAN acknowledges the difficulties:

You ask the critical question: where does religious belief come from? There are literally millions of Jews who are religious. Some are fervent Orthodox Jews. They have no hesitation believing that God revealed the Torah to Moses on Mount

Sinai. Convinced that God chose the Jews as his special people, they devotedly and devoutly observe the 613 commandments.

Moses reports back

'Usury's fine and there's plenty of wiggle room on killing, but, sorry, He still insists on the anti-adultery clause.'

The vast majority of these fervent believers were profoundly influenced by the observant Jewish environment in which they grew up. The traditional beliefs they hold were reinforced by the home and religious schools. It is not surprising that they became strictly Orthodox Jews like their parents and grandparents and great-grandparents before them. As a philosopher you may deplore such unquestioning acceptance of traditional Jewish belief. But this seems to be the pattern of religious conviction across the world's religions.

Religious indoctrination is universal. In the Jewish world it shapes the mind of fervent believers. And if you move across the religious spectrum, the same phenomenon occurs. Non-Orthodox Jews too are influenced by their upbringing and education. I am not embarrassed or ashamed to admit I was shaped by the world I grew up in. I am the product of liberal Judaism, and secularism and rationalism. Where did such ideas and ideals come from? Certainly not from within. I am the product of time and circumstance. Had I grown up in India as the son of a devout Hindu, I might well have become a Hindu priest teaching Hinduism in New Delhi.

Instead I am an American rabbi who taught Judaism in a British university. And so it is for Jews world-wide. Many of us have rejected religion altogether. But there are others who identify with the Jewish past and seek to define themselves somewhere along the Jewish religious spectrum. This is not the result of religious or philosophical speculation. We have not thought ourselves into one or other Jewish denomination. Our upbringing, education and environment have moulded us.

2.6 PETER appeals and concludes:

Your comments, Dan – dare I say? – are pretty complacent. 'Some Jews grow committed to their particular Judaism because they were shaped by their nurturing; others rejected it. That's that.' You refreshingly acknowledge that, had you been nurtured as Hindu, you could have extolled Hinduism. I was brought up as Baptist: I did the rejection bit.

Your approach, Dan, seems to imply that someone could argue, 'Well, I was brought up in a family of Nazi antisemites; that justifies me in seeking to exterminate the Jews.' Or 'I was nurtured as a traditional conservative Muslim; that's why I disparage all Jews.'

My simple point is that whatever your upbringing, although it may *cause* your beliefs, it does not thereby *justify* them as true. Further, whatever ancient texts you read or synagogue tales you hear, they are not, in themselves, sufficient to show how you ought morally to live, just as they are not sufficient to show that a divine creator exists.

At times, you have told me of how Judaism speaks to you of 'inescapable mysterious ways in making you who you are'. That sounds wonderful. When I return to Cambridge, I go along to Evensong at King's College, my old college. The soaring music enraptures; mysterious biblical words intrigue. All that is splendid and thought provoking. All that, though, proves nothing about the world's creation, nothing about the existence of God who demands – deserves? – worship and nothing about Moses and the commandments.

'Judaism', as with 'Jewishness', is manifestly a family resemblance term. Some members of that family insist that only they capture religious truth. In view of the different Judaisms, though, humility should surely block fierce commitments to particular Judaic models and to Judaism more generally. None of this terribly matters, save for the fact that typically religions impinge on our understanding of how we ought to live and how others ought to live – as we are next to discuss.

Mullings

Dan asks:
  Is religious belief a leap of faith – or something else?

Peter asks:
  Do Orthodox Jews and Reform Jews speak the same language regarding Judaism?

Chapter Three
What is Jewish morality?

3.1 DAN writes:

Let me begin this discussion by quoting the law about masturbation in the *Shulhan Arukh* – the Code of Jewish Law – that we have already met:

> It is forbidden to discharge semen in vain. This is more severe than any of the other prohibitions of the Torah. Those who masturbate and discharge semen in vain not only violate a severe prohibition, but also should be placed under a ban of ostracism. Concerning them [Isaiah 1.15] states: 'your hands are full of blood,' it is equivalent to murder.

I wonder what you think of this. As a Reform Jew, I believe it is utterly extreme and totally irrelevant in modern society, yet the Orthodox are compelled to follow the *Shulhan Arukh* in its entirety.

Jewish ethics is traditionally understood as consisting of all the moral laws in the *Shulhan Arukh*. They are of divine origin and must be obeyed.

There is no scope for dispute. Today, Orthodox Jews throughout the globe regard the laws as the foundation of Jewish living. But not surprisingly, that is not the case in the non-Orthodox world. Reform, Conservative and Reconstructionist Jews are not bound by either biblical law or rabbinic injunctions. They have set aside the doctrine of *Torah MiSinai* – the belief that God revealed the Torah to Moses on Mt Sinai. Instead of rigorously observing the mitzvot (commandments), they select those moral teachings which they regard as spiritually meaningful.

It is striking how far the non-Orthodox have departed from the Jewish heritage in matters of ethics. For example, it is a cardinal principle in Reform Judaism that homosexuality is morally acceptable. Today, Reform rabbis conduct gay and lesbian marriages. And as far as non-observant Jews are concerned, the *Shulhan Arukh* with its multifarious laws regarding all aspects of Jewish life has lost its relevance. This is not to say that non-observant Jews lack moral principles. Rather they have freed themselves from the restraints of the past. They follow their consciences about what is right and wrong.

3.2 PETER muses:

In musing upon morality, masturbation rarely comes to mind; such sexual activity requires contexts of more alluring orders. It is, though, a good example of sexual taboos mingling with morality; even the great non-Jewish Enlightenment philosopher Immanuel Kant, fine advocate of rationality, believed masturbation to be morally worse than suicide. He gave reasons: both suicide and masturbation are wrong because they are 'against Nature', but, with the latter, we also gain pleasure from what is wrong.

By 'Jewish morality', Dan, you are presumably talking about morality espoused by Jews committed to a Judaism of some ilk. As you say, the Orthodox, as with other conservative religious believers, ground their morality in ancient texts and traditions. That grounding is as crazy as insisting, because of ancient texts, that the Sun orbits the Earth. More accurately, that would be crazy, unless we held that those texts derived directly from God – who would judge us badly if we challenged them. And that is the problem.

That is the problem because how can we, through rational discussion and appeals to fellow feeling, dislodge beliefs that, according to believers, derive from divine omnipotence? Challenging their beliefs is, from their perspective, to be challenging God – and what chance has a humble philosopher, even a Reform rabbi, in winning against divinity? If God tells you to murder Egypt's first born, you had better do so. You had better do so, unless you have a sense of morality independently of God's apparent commands. It is to

Jewish ethics?

A Jewish man, sitting in a delicatessen, notices a Jewish funeral. Two hearses go by with a man behind them walking a dog on a leash. A line of hundreds of men follows him. Curious, the man goes over to the person walking the dog. When he reaches him, he expresses his surprise for he has never seen a Jewish funeral with two hearses.

The man with the dog tells him how one hearse is for his wife who yelled at him and was then attacked and killed by the dog he is walking right here with him. The second hearse, he explains, is for his mother-in-law, who was attempting to help his wife, and was also attacked and killed by the dog.

The man from the deli offers his condolences, and the two share a moment of male connectedness, then the man from the deli asks if he can borrow the dog. The mourner replies, 'Get in line.'

that sense, it seems, that you appeal, Dan, when turning to conscience and fresh interpretations of scriptures.

'With one bound, we are free, free from ancient texts' – that is the feeling you give, Dan, when promoting conscience as the source of moral truth. Sadly, things are not so easy. That little voice of conscience, be it Jewish, Christian or Islamic, or indeed Heathen, leads to all manner of horrors. Some, in 'full conscience', insist that contraception be forbidden, sexual promiscuity is evil and women should be veiled in public.

'My conscience tells me' can be as dangerously table-thumping as the *'Shulhan Arukh* tells me'. How do you determine which injunctions of conscience should be followed?

3.3 DAN continues:

For Orthodox Jews morality is derived from God's revelation to Moses on Mt Sinai. As I noted, the 613 commandments and the rabbinic interpretation of these laws constitute the basis for living an authentically religious life in accordance with God's will. Morality flows directly from the Almighty.

The great advantage of contemporary non-Orthodox Jewish movements such as Reform Judaism is that they revere the Jewish heritage, but at the same time seek to embrace insights of modern knowledge and scientific discovery. With regard to morality, most modern Jews no longer feel bound by the religious strictures of the past. Progressive Jews seek to preserve the Jewish heritage, while recognizing the importance of modernizing the tradition. They select those elements of the Jewish heritage which they regard as spiritually meaningful. But by what criteria do they make such a selection?

That is the question you keep pressing. In general, the approach is unsystematic and often inconsistent. Frequently, appeals are made to such principles as justice, benevolence and egalitarianism.

Let me give an example. In the past and currently within strictly Orthodox circles, there are severe restrictions concerning female participation in Jewish religious life. Women are not allowed to serve as rabbis or cantors; they are not allowed to be witnesses in legal proceedings; they are not permitted to initiate a divorce; they must sit separately from men during religious services. The Orthodox defend such restrictions by pointing out that women have a separate but elevated role in Jewish life. Non-Orthodox critics contend that such limitations treat women as inferior to men. Here, then, is a battle of assumptions.

For the Orthodox, God is the source of morality. Progressive Jews, though, appeal to ethical principles to determine the relevance of traditional Jewish guidance. In doing so they have set themselves against thousands of years of Jewish teaching. Unsurprisingly, Orthodox critics vehemently protest that non-Orthodox Jews have uprooted the foundations of the faith, and that what they believe and practice is a scandal and blasphemy.

3.4 PETER battles on:

Years ago, Woolworths, before its demise, allowed customers to 'mix and match' chocolates, candies and nuts to build up a bag of the aforementioned for purchase. Jews, in assessing morality, seem to mix and match.

Turning first to the Orthodox, they ground morality on two highly doubtful beliefs. First, the Hebrew Bible correctly says what God commands. How, though, can that be assessed? Is it not likely that mistakes would have arisen? Even if God is infallible, human beings – hearers, scribes, interpreters – are not. Even the Orthodox argue over interpretation.

Secondly, God's commandments, it is believed, are morally meritorious. My response is: Really? God, at one stage, demanded the killing of Egypt's first born; the Hebrew Bible tells of many horrendous deeds ordered by God. Dan, you have cited instances where God is still taken to demand wayward ways – ways that offend ideals of sexual equality and freedom in sexual activities. Whether those are God's mistakes or interpretational mistakes does not terribly matter; what matters is that we spot them as mistakes, without relying on God.

Turning to Progressive Jews – well, Dan, you speak of their modernization of Judaism through scientific discoveries, ethical principles and the spiritually meaningful found in Judaism. How, though, do you select from that mish-mash and how does that selection inform you of what is right? You need to explain.

My hunch is that you use a medley of values – consistency, fellow-feeling, courage, honesty, fairness – yet none having any essential reliance on Judaism. Once that medley is recognized, Christians, Muslims, Jews, Hindus, Humanists, Atheists – *human beings* – will have much agreement over morality. Some disagreements will remain, but they should arise neither because one is a Reform Jew, another a Christian, a third a Muslim, nor because one interpretation of an ancient text vies with an opposing interpretation. Disagreements properly arise because values are not easily measured against each other – and facts are often uncertain.

Yes, Jews have distinctive traditions. Yes, Jews face horrors of antisemitism and perplexities of their Israeli homeland. Once we have moved from versions of ultra-Orthodox and Orthodox Judaism, though, is there anything distinctively Jewish about Jewish morality?

3.5 DAN wrestles with Peter's questions:

How can one assess the Orthodox belief in the *Torah MiSinai*? Reform Judaism offers a compelling critique. It is based on an understanding of the composition of the Pentateuch. Ever since the nineteenth century, scholars – engaged in 'biblical criticism' – have written extensively about that text. They have concluded that the Five Books of Moses are a composite work written over centuries by ancient Hebrews. The Torah is thus not Mosaic in the sense of Moses as the author. It is a mosaic produced by many writers and editors. It is a composite work reflecting the religious beliefs of generations of Jewish writers.

The implications of this altered perspective are wide-reaching for the Jewish faith. It is no longer credible to think that Moses wrote Genesis, Exodus, Leviticus, Numbers and Deuteronomy, or that he recorded the 613 laws. Instead, these books and commandments are products of particular circumstances and reflect the then cultural conditions. Of course, the Orthodox reject the findings of these biblical scholars. For the Orthodox, it is an article of faith that God revealed the Torah and that biblical law manifests divine will. Non-Orthodox Jews do not agree.

Now, you are right to point out that this leads to an uncomfortable situation. How is one to know if any of the 613 commandments is of divine origin? Unsurprisingly, some non-Orthodox Jews believe that some laws, such as the Ten Commandments, were willed by God. If those commandments, why not others? Ultimately it is all a matter of subjective preference.

The same subjectivity applies to the choice of other criteria for accepting or rejecting biblical law. Non-Orthodox Jews frequently appeal to such notions as 'the dictates of conscience'. Yet, in the end, both the choice of such criteria and their application is personal and subjective. This has inevitably resulted in a totally chaotic approach to Jewish ethics in circles beyond that of the Orthodox.

3.6 PETER condemns, then softens – a little:

Dan, I warm to your fun with 'mosaic', but I am far from warming to your morality as 'personal and subjective choice'. That is wrong – dangerously so. I hardly need to remind you of the horrendous choices people have made about the right and wrong.

I may have a personal preference for the red dress rather than the blue; when romance arises, I remain permitted (I trust) to prefer raven-haired to blonde – even women to men. I cannot, though, choose to make nineteen an even number or, in my case, to run a mile, let alone in under four minutes.

I also cannot choose to make killing an innocent girl against her will a rightful deed. Such a deed is wrong, full stop. It is no matter of choice whether honesty and compassion should be admired over dishonesty and callousness. Personal subjective choice typically can no more determine what is morally praiseworthy and despicable, than it can determine whether nineteen is a prime number, Everest is a mountain and his dress is too tight. Many morally grey areas and moral dilemmas undoubtedly exist. That no more shows there are no clear instances of right and wrong than indeterminate shades between red and orange show there are no clear instances of red and orange.

The Hebrew Bible is a fertile text, presenting the Garden of Eden, the Tree of Knowledge, a serpent and the odd apple; there are the tribulations of Job, something about Lot and salt and adages such as 'pride cometh before a fall' and 'do not oppress a stranger'. We have the erotic Song of Songs and Ecclesiastes with meditations on life's follies. Yes, Dan, that rich Judaic culture provokes reflection. That is also true of Greek gods, Hindu myths and the Tao. It is too easy, though, to say that Judaic scriptures are full of profound ethical insight and meaning. We need to assess them, case by case.

Neither 'the Torah tells us' nor 'that's my subjective preference' is good justification for what we morally ought to do. Just as it is the reality of my biology that prevents my running a mile and the nature of numbers that blocks the number nineteen from being even, so it is the reality of right and wrong that should guide our actions.

> **Mullings**
>
> Dan asks:
> > Are moral values absolute, or relative? How can one know?
>
> Peter asks:
> > Are religious Jews best placed for determining what is of moral value in the Hebrew Bible?

Chapter Four

Do Jews not care about animal welfare?

4.1 DAN writes:

A common criticism of Jews levelled by antisemites is that Judaism fosters an unethical attitude toward animals. During the Nazi period, such criticism was a central theme. In Nazi propaganda, kashrut (a set of Jewish laws regulating slaughter) was deliberately misrepresented so as to tie in with claims that Jews engaged in perverse ritual killings of humans for their blood.

The truth, however, is that Judaism teaches that animals are part of God's creation and should be treated with compassion. This principle is referred to in rabbinic sources as 'tzar baalei chayim' (the prohibition on causing pain to any living creature). According to the Talmud, Jews are not to cause suffering to any animals – such a view is based on Bible stories which use kindness to animals as a demonstration of the virtues of various individuals.

This does not mean, however, that Jews are required to be vegetarians. Rather, the tradition asserts that animals can be used for human needs. But their slaughter must be done in the most humane way possible. Such a view is based on the scriptural claim that God has given human beings the right to control all non-human life. Consequently, Jews are permitted to use animals for food and clothing, and to provide parchment on which to write the Torah. But they must be killed in such a way as to cause the least amount of suffering.

Of course, it can be argued that the principle of 'tzar baalei chayim' does not go far enough. If animals are not to suffer, then ideally they should not be killed for food. Although vegetarianism has not been the ethical norm within Judaism, it has invariably been accepted as the best ethical opinion, one that more clearly approximates to the original will of the Creator. Indeed, some Jewish scholars have insisted that ethical vegetarianism lies at the heart of the Torah. One highly respected rabbinic scholar, Abraham Isaac Kook, maintained that the biblical constraints concerning killing are themselves preparation for a state of higher ethical awareness.

4.2 PETER first responds:

Dan, you mention how the Jewish attitude to animals can be linked to antisemitism. My guess is that many, many antisemites have little knowledge or interest in the Judaic approach to animal welfare. By the way, I use 'animal' as an abbreviation for 'non-human animal'.

Many antisemites are Muslims who lack much concern for animal welfare. After all, Muslims typically oppose any stunning of animals prior to slaughter; animals attending the Islamic abattoir certainly seem to undergo unnecessary suffering. Indeed – and in word – many antisemites, religious or no, are probably as insensitive to animal suffering as to Jewish suffering through antisemitism. Individuals who attack Jews may well overlap with those who torment dogs for fun or who weirdly drive into the countryside to mutilate horses. I resist – and hence fail to resist – drawing attention to those British traditionalists who enjoy chasing foxes to be gnawed alive, and finally to death, by 'tally ho' hounds, and those Americans who go off to Africa to delight in killing large game – elephants, giraffes – for entertainment and show-off.

The particular animal welfare problem for Jews is, of course, the kosher prohibition on stunning prior to slaughter, akin to the Islamic prohibition just mentioned, regarding the provision of halal meat. One question, then, is whether it is true that Jews and Judaism require a special way of slaughtering animals. Another is: if they do, does that way in fact lead to more suffering than pre-stunning ways?

Assuming that meat needs to be on offer, should our treatment of animals be determined by certain religious texts, traditions and interpretations – or ought our treatment be that which causes the least possible amount of animal suffering? Fundamentally, the matter comes down to whether concern for animal welfare should be grounded in what is best for the animals 'from their viewpoint' or in so-called divine injunctions about the human use of animals. I go with the former.

4.3 DAN retorts:

As a Reform Jew, I do not feel obliged to follow kashrut. Unlike the Orthodox, I do not believe the food laws in the Torah were revealed by God to Moses. It may well be true, though, that Jewish laws regarding slaughter were originally formulated to reduce animal suffering.

There is no doubt that both the Bible and rabbinic sources contain a wide range of legislation concerning animal welfare. Nonetheless, I agree with you that the Jewish heritage should not be the final arbiter of moral concern.

'Impossible?' you say

Hymie walks into his synagogue – with a dog. The shammes comes up and says, 'This is a House of Worship, Hymie; you can't bring a dog in here.'

'What do you mean I can't?' says Hymie, 'Look at him, he's as Jewish a dog as they come.'

The shammes sees that the dog has a tallis bag round its neck and Hymie now says, 'Benjamin, daven for me.'

Benjamin stands on his hind legs, does a 'Woof, woof, woof,' opens the tallis bag, takes out a kippa and puts it on his head. 'Woof, woof,' goes Benjamin, putting the tallis round his neck. There are more 'woof's as he now takes out a siddur and starts to pray, rocking from side to side.

'That's brilliant,' says the shammes, 'Incredible. You must get him on TV – you could make millions.'

'You speak to him,' says Hymie. 'He wants to be a doctor.'

For Jews, the tradition provides a framework for understanding our relation to animals, but we must also take into account scientific research about animal suffering. Thus, I believe that we Jews must reassess the traditional method of slaughtering.

Is pre-stunning the most humane form of slaughter? Not surprisingly, Orthodox apologists maintain *a priori* that the Jewish method of slaughtering is the most humane. They are vehement in their condemnation of animal welfare organizations which contend that Jewish law should be superseded by a more humane approach. But my co-religionists are wrong. They simply fail to take into account the animal research. Jews are not obliged to eat meat. It is a concession for them to do so. So, if Orthodox Jews believe they should only eat meat that has been ritually slaughtered, it would be better for them to give up eating meat altogether.

Which brings me to your own view. You are a humanist. You believe that human action should be guided by the highest moral principles. In your estimation, our ethical attitudes should not be dictated by religious traditions. Rather our actions should be based on rational considerations. In this light, I think vegetarianism is a most worthy attitude to adopt. This was not always my view. I became a vegetarian many years ago after writing a book *After Noah: Theology and the Liberation of*

Animals. I asked myself the question: could I eat my beloved cat? Of course, the answer was 'No'. And I saw that if this applied to our cat, then why not to cows and sheep and all sentient creatures?

4.4 PETER ponders further:

Your response, as ever, Dan, casts me into questioning seas – though praise be to your cat, for leading you away from the beef and the lamb. Your love of the beef and lamb was insufficient to tempt you into feline dining.

You oppose the eating of sentient mammals; I hope that you do not, then, lapse into eating fish, but maybe you go for the prawns, despite their offence to kashrut. I wonder if you wear leather shoes (or leather anything else) and if you eat eggs and drink milk, despite the bad times that dairy cows, hens, ducks *et al* appear to undergo. Today's shampoos and cosmetics indirectly derive from animal testing that inflicted pains on rabbits, or similar, tightly en-caged. Animal experimentation – chimps often have a bad time – continues in the quest for new medical treatments, primarily for human benefit.

Do Jews not care about animal welfare?

I expand, so to speak. Most good things in our lives are founded on pains of the past, the distant past as well as a few months, a few weeks, even a few days ago. Benefits include those of highways across the States, sewers in cities and magnificent cathedrals throughout Europe. Look closely and we see slavery and exploitation of the poor that, one way or another, are the foundations of such projects. Horrors and injustices hover behind the Pyramids, the Golden Gate and Britain's Tower of London – and today's inexpensive clothing on sale – in which we delight.

Here is an ancient Greek saw, 'All things conspire'. We benefit directly and indirectly from a vast range of sufferings undergone by human beings and animals. The 'we' includes numerous people, both Jews and atheists, both Christians and Muslims.

Returning specifically to animals, most Jews and non-Jews sail on seas of inconsistency, closing their eyes to how they both benefit from past animal suffering and perpetuate it. I am among the guiltily inconsistent. Of course, as a matter of fact, some religions, Jainism, for example, are much kinder to animals than others. That outcome is good, but it would be much better were our treatment of animals grounded in what is best for them, *for their sake.*

I should be content with the second best of good animal treatment purely for religious reasons or for human health reasons – if animals have a better time. The worry is that, if we succumb to accepting religious reasons for respecting animals, we are vulnerable to the religious who demand that we should also accept their religious reasons, for example, for discriminating against homosexuals or treating women as lacking the rights of men.

4.5 DAN replies:

You point out that both of us are inconsistent. Animal welfare is a key moral issue for you, as for me. You do not have a cat like I do, so your views are not based on personal experience. There is no fluffy creature who comes into view and compels you to think through your ideas. Nonetheless, you quite rightly point out that animal suffering should not take place if it can be avoided. In this, we are agreed.

I perceive the inconsistencies in my viewpoint. You are not a vegetarian despite your recognition that animals suffer as a result of the meat industry. Although I am generally vegetarian, I do eat fish. I do have leather goods. You are right to criticize me for a lack of rigour. Vegans score higher than I do. But what are you and I to do? Does the fact that we are inconsistent mean that we should ignore the suffering of animals? Surely not.

I try to do my best, as I am sure you do. Each of us has to set our moral compass. At the very least, we should be sensitive to the needs of animals, and attempt to find a way through the moral problems. The difficulties of adopting an entirely consistent position should not blind us to the significance of this ethical problem. In other words, it is important that we imperfectly 'muddle through', a path that you often recommend, Peter.

Those who castigate religious Jews have embarked on a moral crusade, often ignoring the numerous ways in which animals are forced to suffer in the food industry. Is such a critique of

Jewish religious practice in fact a subtle form of Jew-hatred? I have witnessed the same phenomenon when speaking to non-Jewish audiences about the Israel-Palestine conflict. Frequently opponents of Israeli policies bitterly condemn the Israeli government for its treatment of Palestinians. They are vehement in their denunciations. But condemning the Jewish state, they overlook the terrible regimes around the world whose actions are as bad or worse.

4.6 PETER concludes:

With regard to your musing (again) that opposition to kosher slaughter is a subtle form of Jew-hatred – I assume you use that as a variant for 'antisemitism' – well, Hitler's prohibition was doubtless a manifestation of such hatred, but hardly subtle – and most people today who actively target it also condemn Islamic practices, factory farming, fox hunting and animal vivisection.

Kashrut – eating food according to strict rabbinic law – strikes many people, including some Jews, as quaint. In Roger Horowitz's *Kosher USA*, I read with amusement Orthodox anguishes when first encountering unfamiliar foods. Allowable

– kosher – fish includes halibut and carp, but the sturgeon with its ganoid scales – kosher? After some deliberation, 'No'. Coca-Cola posed problems for the Orthodox Union, the US kosher certifying agency. Many of us smile at such deliberations – as I did, when in Jerusalem, faced with paper plates at breakfast, to keep within rabbinic law.

Traditions have the value of holding people together, whether the traditions involve naked prancing for the Winter Solstice or Jewish demands to separate meat and dairy tableware. That value, though, should be overridden when it necessitates unnecessary suffering of others, even if the others are mere beasts of the field. Let us not pretend that slaughterhouse practices are anything other than gruesome; but let us not pretend that Orthodox Jewish and Islamic ritual slaughter is no worse. The evidence is in; it is worse.

Religious commitments are burdensome. If kosher requirements are so supremely important, then, instead of seeking exemptions from slaughterhouse welfare regulations, Jews should turn vegetarian – or revisit rabbinic law, giving higher priority to the Talmud's rejection of causing pain to any living creature. Sincere commitment to Judaism should not be made easier at the expense of animal suffering.

None of our observations solves the problem of how to treat animals; so, I am pleased that you conclude with my much-deployed mantra 'we muddle through'. The best we can do is to do our best – and that may well be far from the best.

Mullings

Dan asks:
  Do animals have rights?

Peter asks:
  Should Judaic scripture and tradition alone ever determine how we morally ought to treat animals?

Chapter Five

Zionism: 'Next year, in Jerusalem' – but whose Jerusalem?

5.1 DAN writes:

You might think that Zionism was initially embraced by Jews worldwide. But this was not so. The early Zionists such as Theodor Herzl constituted a tiny minority. In *The Jewish State* (1896), Herzl argued that Jews will never be safe in the lands where they live. The solution to the problem of Jew-hatred is for the Jewish people to have their own country.

The vast majority of Jews, however, remained indifferent to this plea. Strictly Orthodox Jews viewed Zionism as a pernicious heresy. According to traditional Judaism, they insisted, Jews must wait for the Messiah to arrive to lead the Jewish people to their ancient homeland. Throughout the world, Orthodox leaders denounced the Zionists and branded Zionism a heresy.

Reform Jews were similarly united against the Zionists. What is necessary, they argued, is for Jews to assimilate into the societies in which they live, moderate their religious practices, and integrate into the mainstream of modern life. In this way, antisemitism will naturally fade away. Jewish socialists too rejected Zionism as an ethnocentric ideology. In their view, Jews must work together to reform society on socialist lines.

In time, however, Zionism became more widely accepted in the Jewish world. Across the religious spectrum Jews increasingly embraced the idea that persecuted Jews needed a safe haven in the Holy Land. The Holocaust reinforced the belief that Jewish existence was precarious. With the creation of Israel in 1948 the vast majority of Jews adopted Zionism as fundamental to Jewish existence.

From its inception, Zionism adopted the view that Jewry must return to their ancestral homeland. Arabs living in Palestine, however, viewed the Jews as usurpers of their land. Determinedly and repeatedly they fought against the Zionists. In response, Zionists argued that Palestine belonged to the Jewish people. For over a thousand years they occupied the Holy Land, and hence it belonged to the Jewish nation.

5.2 PETER responds:

People have an understandable need to be safe and secure. As you usefully tell me, Dan, to satisfy that need, Reform Jews early on saw assimilation as the means; others, later on, saw separation. It is an empirical question which is more likely to secure the desirable end. Assimilate or separate? Whichever path is followed, there are dangers: we witness them for Jews in Israel; we witness them for Jews outside Israel. Within and without, insecurities arise. We both know that.

To live here?

Max Goldberg was a good, well-respected elderly man from New York. He felt that death was close and asked his sons to take him to the Holy Land, to die there and be buried in Jerusalem.

The loving sons did as he asked, brought him to Jerusalem, put him in a hospital and waited for death to come.

Once in Jerusalem, Max began to feel better and better and after a few weeks was again strong and full of life. He called his sons, 'Quickly, take me back to New York.'

The sons were disappointed. 'Father, how come? You said you want to die in the Holy Land and be buried in Jerusalem!'

'Yes,' answered Max, 'to die here is fine – but to live here?'

Factors other than safety and security come into play. Many people, be they Orthodox Jews or Progressives – Catholics or Protestants; the Mayas of Guatemala or the Maoris of New Zealand – see their identity as essentially tied to their culture, religion, ethnicity or geography. For many Jews, religious or not, assimilation risks identity loss. Of course, some would be prepared to suffer that loss; a few may welcome it. Many, though, favour separation; they favour a Jewish state, distinct and distinctive.

Diversity has value. We should surely welcome a world that contains both Colorado's Rocky Mountains and the Plains of Kansas. Rainforests are desirable, so too are arid deserts, yet also England's Lake District and East Anglian Fens. The diversity of cultures and identities have similar appeal.

Preservation of identity, with security, tips the balance in favour of a Jewish state as an optional home. Why not, though, form the state in the Iberian Peninsula, once home of the Sephardi Jews, or in Eastern Europe where the Ashkenazi Jews founded communities – or in the United States, already the home of millions of Jews?

The answer is: Jewish identity is tied to the ancestral homeland of millennia ago, not the European homes only a few centuries ago. A particular piece of land has significance as the Jewish 'Holy Land', that land roughly between the Jordan

River and Mediterranean Sea, where the Book of Books came into view, where the Jews became God's chosen people – a land that, for the Jews, is the 'Promised Land' containing Jerusalem, that holiest of cities. For many Jews, that significance, though, led not at all to calls for a Jewish state; such Jews opposed such a man-made state – a stance which today is apparently deemed antisemitic by mainstream Jewry.

Today's strong support for Israel – Zionism – is grounded in certain Jewish beliefs about Jewish identity, strengthened by awareness of the horrendous sufferings of the Holocaust. Jerusalem is 'home', despite – paradoxically – for hundreds of years it being no home at all for most Jews and their recent ancestors. Dan, what, then, can we make of such 'home coming'?

5.3 DAN thinks on:

Peter, you are right. Orthodox, Reform and socialist critics of Zionism at the end of the nineteenth century would now be viewed as antisemitic or at least as self-hating Jews. It is paradoxical, though, that the Zionist solution to the problem of antisemitism, with the creation of Israel, no longer looks credible. Zionists like Herzl were convinced that if Jews possessed a state of their own, they would be able to protect themselves from a hostile gentile world. In one sense this is true. Israel has become a safe-haven for Jews who are under threat in the diaspora. All Jews have the right to settle in Israel under the Law of Return. Yet, the creation of a Jewish state has fermented a new virulent form of antisemitism or Judeophobia: namely, Arab antisemitism.

You raise the question about a Jewish state's rightful location. Possibly you are unaware that this was a vexed question during the early Zionist Congresses. Sympathetic to the Zionist cause, the then British Colonial Secretary, Joseph Chamberlain, suggested to Herzl that a Jewish homeland could be established in Uganda. Fearful of the plight of Russian Jewry at the end of the nineteenth century, Herzl was prepared to accept the proposal.

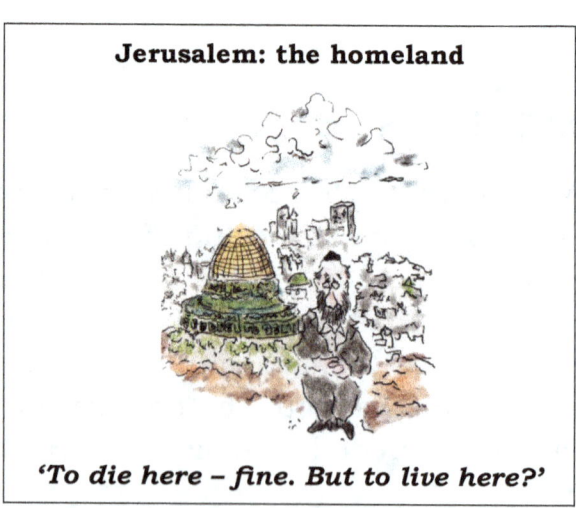

Jerusalem: the homeland

'To die here – fine. But to live here?'

The Uganda Plan was presented to the Zionist Congress. Russian Jewish delegates, however, vehemently opposed the scheme which they regarded as a betrayal of Zionism – and it was duly formally rejected.

Instead, Zionists remained determined to establish a Jewish state in the Holy Land, their ancestral home. Ahad Ha-Am, a late nineteenth-century Hebrew essayist and founder of cultural Zionism, was prophetic about the Arab suffering that would result. Herzl and others were misguided to think that Palestine was 'a land of no people, for a people of no land.' That was never so.

The key problem is that the Jewish and the Palestinian narratives are utterly different. For the Jewish people, Israel is a central focus of concern: in a post-Holocaust age the Jewish state is perceived as vital to Jewish survival. For the Palestinians, the Zionists are perceived as colonial oppressors who have stolen their land. The Palestinian protests in Gaza in May 2018 are a reflection of such a view. How is such a fundamental conflict of viewpoints to be resolved?

5.4 PETER muses further:

My immediate response to your question is 'I have no idea'. My reflective response is, 'Forget'.

Memory loss has value. A friend would comment that his wife remembers his transgressions 'from the Middle Ages'; he would remind her of the United States' Statute of Limitation that forbids the prosecution of actions so ancient. How far back should one go?

Often, it is difficult to forget; often it is important to remember – especially important when one's identity is at stake. Hence, my 'forget' solution is no solution, though it may remind us to resist letting the past, especially the distant past, burden the present too much – but how much is 'too much'? Of course, it is far from easy to forget when blood and suffering are to the fore; a notable example was Israel's fierce military response, seemingly excessive, to the Palestinian protests in May 2018 that you mention, with thousands of impoverished Gazan Palestinians injured and quite a few killed.

The past burdens heavily when it leads to territorial conflicts: 'to whom does this land *really* belong?' Remember: many lands have been acquired by conquest; outcomes accepted. We have the 1815 Congress of Vienna, the 1919 Treaty of Versailles and the 1947 Paris Peace Treaties. Europe's political map today is very different compared with maps a century or so ago. Palestinians are aggrieved by the Zionists; they should also complain about how some Palestinian land was annexed by Jordan. Poles and Germans could demand return of some Eastern lands now in Russia.

I doubt the existence of clear criteria for determining which nation should own which lands. Perhaps, for the sake of justice, it is better to consider how well a land is governed rather than who controlled it thousands of years ago or even a few decades ago. Regarding any territory under a nation's control, we should ask: what is permitted under that control? With that in mind, it is worth reflecting that when East Jerusalem, with the Old City, rested in Jordanian hands during the 1950s and 1960s, Jews were barred from their holiest of sites, the Western Wall. Now, under Israeli jurisdiction, Muslims have access to their Islamic shrine, the Dome of the Rock on the Temple Mount. That contrast is telling.

Of course, many factors are important when assessing how government control promotes or violates people's flourishing. What is permitted regarding freedom of speech, voting rights and movement between countries? Far better to anguish on those matters and try to improve things, rather than wringing hands about which historical invasion or territorial agreement was – or was not – justified.

5.5 DAN objects:

It is unrealistic to ask either Jews or Palestinians to forget the past. For both peoples, the past is critical. It is the past that shapes the present and determines the future. I view the matter very differently from you. Jews and Palestinians should be fully aware not only of their own past, but of the past of their enemies. There is a fierce clash of perspectives about the Holy Land. Any solution demands openness and sympathy. We must listen to each other and be willing to make enormous and painful compromises.

The central problem that bedevils all discussions about the Palestine-Israeli conflict is that there are two fundamentally different narratives about the region's history. I have spoken at many conferences with Jews and Palestinians present. It is always the same. Jewish participants anxiously explain the necessity of a Jewish state. They emphasize how, through centuries, Jewry has been subject to contempt and persecution. They stress how the Holocaust has cast a shadow over the Jewish community. They describe the bravery of Zionist settlers in the face of Arab efforts to drive Jews into the sea. They blame Palestinians for their intransigence.

Palestinians, on the other hand, stress that the indigenous Arab population in Palestine was betrayed by the British, the Balfour Declaration being the product of British imperialism. Jews, they point out, initially constituted only about ten per cent of the population of nineteenth-century Palestine. Yet gradually the Jewish community increased in size with the aim of driving Arabs out of their lands. The Zionists, they state, had a single goal: the creation of a Jewish state with millions of Jewish citizens.

These two conflicting narratives are presented with heartfelt passion. Both sides are convinced by their arguments. And the tragedy is that they are both right.

5.6 PETER concludes:

Pay attention, dear Dan. Although I floated the idea of 'memory loss', it was rejected by me for memory can be important for one's identity; and preserving identity is often valuable. Of course, regarding some identities we urge eradication: we ought not to value preserving identities grounded in traditions of slave-owning, animal cruelty or greed encouraged by global banking.

As you stress, Dan, today's Palestinian and Zionist identities clash; well, they clash territorially. It is as if they are both looking at the same duck/rabbit drawing: Palestinians see only duck; Zionists see only rabbit – or rabbi, if I dare remind you of your opening chapter, Dan.

Camel Confused

'Is that a duck – or a rabbit – at my feet?'

The duck/rabbit analogy suggests that there is no 'right way' of seeing the history and identity of Jews and Palestinians. True, there are many undisputed historical facts: Jerusalem was mainly Jewish until the wars of the first century, when the Romans expelled the Jews; the 1947 United Nations' resolution partitioned Britain's territory under the Palestinian mandate into one Jewish, one Arab; today's United States strongly supports Israel politically and economically. There are, though, different ways of seeing the meaning and moral implications of such facts. That is why conflicts between Palestinians and Jews are of the duck/rabbit ilk.

In April 2018, as marked by the Hebrew calendar, Israeli Jews – and many outside of Israel – celebrated the seventieth anniversary of Israel's foundation. For the Palestinians, a few days later in May, that was the seventieth anniversary of the 'Nakba' (the catastrophe, as they understandably see it), when 700,000 Palestinians were driven from their homes by the Israelis. Their commemorations of that disaster (for them) have families brandishing house keys, symbolizing their homes now under Israeli occupation. Regarding what happened seventy years ago, we have again the duck/rabbit conflict in ways of seeing.

Amongst the Palestinians there are the complexities of diverse groupings – Hamas, Fatah, Hezbollah and the Palestinian authorities – with varying readings of Islam and secularism, though all are opposed to the Jewish State of Israel.

Of course, many Jews living in Israel and many Palestinians living in and around Israel want peace, but there are important asymmetries in leaderships. Many Islamic conservatives, relying on certain interpretations of the Qur'an, apparently want to drive the Jews into the sea, whereas Judaism's conservatives have no reciprocal aquatic aims.

Both sides seek to justify a right to Jerusalem and contested lands. There is, though, more to morality than rights. Values sometimes trump non-violation of rights – values such as generosity, compassion, benevolence. Maybe the starving child has no 'right' to my food, yet it would be callous for me to insist on what is rightfully mine; I ought to be generous and share. A British supermarket sought to prosecute a hungry man who trespassed on its property, taking some discarded food snacks put out as rubbish. The supermarket acted within its rights, yet manifested no morality, no concern for the plight of others.

There is, then, the important difficulty – both practical and moral – of how to open people's eyes to the plight of others. That has startling resonance when the Holocaust comes to the fore, as it does next.

Mullings

Dan asks:
  Has the creation of Israel solved the problem of Jew-hatred or made things worse?

Peter asks:
  Does talk of 'rights' hinder solving the problem of who should control Jerusalem?

Chapter Six

Does the Holocaust make Israel's existence a special case?

6.1 DAN hesitates:

I am not sure that the Holocaust makes Israel a special case, but it has certainly had a profound impact on Zionist ideology. A key element in the growth of Zionist aspirations was the rise of Nazi Germany. In the eyes of many Jews the promise of emancipation and liberation appeared to be a false hope. With the onset of World War II, Zionist aspirations intensified despite Arab opposition. Once images of the concentration camps were released and news of the destruction of six million Jews became widely known, world Jewry united in support for a Jewish homeland.

The Holocaust has thus cast a shadow over modern Jewish life. Israel is now perceived by Jews as of critical importance in assuring their continuation. Only a small minority of Jews now oppose its founding. At the margin of Jewish society, they constitute an insignificant element of modern Jewish life.

You might ask what the impact of the Holocaust has been for Judaism. It has, of course, become extremely difficult for many Jews to believe that God will stand by his people in times of disaster. Increasingly a void exists where once the Jewish people experienced God's presence. As a result, modern Israel has been invested with many of the attributes previously reserved for the Deity. Consequently, in the post-Holocaust world, the traditional conception of a divine redeemer and deliverer has been eclipsed by a policy of Jewish self-protection. It is the Holy Land which is viewed as ultimately capable of providing a safe haven. Israel – not the God of history – is conceived as the protector of the Jewish people.

6.2 PETER ponders:

In view of the Holocaust, and antisemitism over the ages, I warm to your story, Dan, that most Jews of today see Israel as a worldly 'best' substitute for God. Maybe I warm because of my atheism. God's divinity, at least to date, has a poor record of achievement in protecting his chosen people. He could do better – much better. With God out of the frame, what ought to have been the response to the Holocaust?

The Holocaust justified demands that 'something must be done'. That something could have been greater commitment to promoting assimilation, fellow-feeling between Jews and non-Jews, and winning battles against antisemitism. Understandably, that approach struck political players, Jews and non-Jews, as wildly optimistic: Jews needed a home of their own – but where?

The Germans could have accepted collective responsibility for the Nazi horrors; they could have offered up some of their land. The United States is vast; it could have carved out a sanctuary, manifesting generosity. Other European nations could have offered. I am reminded of NIMBY: 'not in my back yard'.

Western powers' determination to 'do something' NIMBY had a fortunate ally – namely, the Jews' historical and religious links to the Holy Land. The combination pointed, almost inevitably, to modern Israel's creation.

Perhaps the Holocaust and sense of Jewish identity make Israel's existence a justified special case. There are, though, other special cases: reflect on those genocidal wars that sought the destruction of the Tutsis, the Selk'nam people and, most recently, the Yazidis. Perhaps Israel's existence is not a special case solely because of the Holocaust and Jewish identity, but because, in addition, it has created another special case: the Palestinians' plight.

Are the Western powers, perhaps with antisemitic tints, guilty of passing the moral buck for the Holocaust to the Palestinians? Whatever the motives, the Jewish parcel has, so to speak, landed in Palestinian hands and lands. Paradoxically, the Palestinians, it seems, are expected to show generosity to the Jews because of Nazi atrocities many miles and some years away.

6.3 DAN reacts:

You raise a central dilemma: most Jews believe that in light of the Holocaust, they need a safe haven. But where? Herzl himself proposed two options: Palestine or Argentina. Argentina, he pointed out, is one of the most fertile countries in the world, extending over a vast area with a small population. On the other hand, Palestine was the Jews' historic homeland. With the second option in mind, he sought to persuade the Ottoman Sultan to allow Jews to return to their ancient land.

Does the Holocaust make Israel's existence a special case? 73

Despite the failure to attain this political objective, Herzl and his fellow Zionists pressed their claim. The 1917 Balfour Declaration was the result. Were the Jews right to claim the land as theirs? Or were Palestinians right to defend their land against foreign aggressors? There are two conflicting narratives, and it is difficult to see whose claims are the most legitimate. To my mind, the great pity is that compromise did not occur at an early stage.

Too generous to the Israelis?

On the sixth day, God turned to the Angels and said, 'Today I am going to create a land called Israel. It will be a land of mountains full of snow, sparkly lakes, forests full of all kinds of trees, and high cliffs overlooking sandy beaches with an abundance of sea life.'

God continued, 'I shall make the land rich so that the inhabitants prosper; I shall call the inhabitants "Israelis", and they shall be known to most people on earth.'

'But Lord,' asked the Angels, 'don't you think you are being too generous to these Israelis?'

'Not really,' God replied, 'just wait and see the neighbours I'm going to give them.'

In the early decades of the twentieth century, a number of Jewish thinkers advocated a binational Jewish-Arab state. This was the view of the Jewish philosopher Martin Buber, who argued that the Jewish people should proclaim its desire to live in peace and brotherhood with the Arab people and to develop the common homeland into a republic in which both peoples would have the possibility of free development. Rejecting the idea of Zionism as just another national movement, he wanted to see the creation of an exemplary society: a society which would not be characterized by Jewish domination. Regrettably, his idea did not materialize.

6.4 PETER muses further in his ignorance:

A binational state of Palestinians and Jews, as you describe, Dan, would seem an obvious solution. 'It is simple, dear Palestinians and Jews, just manifest generosity and empathy.' That, of course, is easy to say, but difficult to do, if you are the Palestinians and Jews affected.

We have bi-fashion states – multi-fashion states – that permit citizens and visitors to wear whatever they like. Some dislike the shabby chic of torn jeans, others the bow tie. I may prefer demure blue dresses; knowing you, Dan, you may prefer skimpy red. We tolerate different tastes; we may even admire rebels of fashion. It matters not at all – *ooops*: that is not quite true. Even the most liberal of multi-fashion states impose restrictions. In Britain, Stephen Gough, 'the naked rambler', is imprisoned for his minimalist garb (socks and shoes only). Customs and corporations impose dress codes. We put up with such minor restrictions.

What matters to many are their traditions, be they religious, ethnic or cultural. In such matters, people are disinclined to put up with restrictions. Some Muslims, for example, demand freedom to engage in their own practices – say, Muslim women to be fully veiled in public – yet also prohibition on the practices of others, such as drawing and displaying cartoons of Muhammad.

Consider the ringmaster. The circus ringmaster permits different acts: clowns, jugglers and young ladies on the trapeze. The *State Ringmaster* permits a plurality of ways of living, be they religious or no, rock bands or string quartets. Conductors, though, differ from ringmasters; all members of the orchestra must play according to the one score. *State Conductors* expect all citizens to live according to the state's determination; they

demand that all sing from the same hymn sheet, often one with a particular, religious tune.

Suppose a secular liberal ringmaster for Israel, providing equally for Jews and Palestinians: we immediately encounter problems. Witness France's controversial ban on full-faced veils worn in public: the ban upsets many Muslims, but not Jews. Were the State Ringmaster to be neither Jewish nor Palestinian, that would offend both Jewish and Palestinian desires for self-determination. Presumably, the religious of both sides would accept God, *Ringmaster Divine*; unfortunately, God as Yahweh is, apparently, somewhat opposed by God as Allah.

Lest we forget, this chapter began with the Holocaust, the Holocaust that convinced many people of the Jewish vulnerability in a world stained by antisemitism. Consequently, Jews sought a state of their own. How could it be their own, if binational? How could it be their own – if not their own?

6.5 DAN reflects:

Who is the ringmaster in modern Israel? If, in the past, the strictly Orthodox had been able to gain power, they would have taken charge over everything. In fact, they only control areas of personal status, setting rules for marriage, conversion and other matters related to religious rights. Orthodox Judaism is the established state religion, but its authority is much limited. Non-Orthodox movements such as Reform Judaism play no role in official Israeli Jewish life.

Because Israel is essentially a secular state, there are severe restrictions on the imposition of Orthodox Jewish law, except in the case of Jewish marriage which is under Orthodox control. For example, all Jews, regardless of their affiliation, are allowed to settle in Israel under the

Law of Return and become citizens. Individuals who have converted to Judaism under the auspices of non-Orthodox religious bodies – and hence viewed as non-Jews by the Orthodox – are treated as Jews by Israel. Persons who have a Jewish father, but no Jewish mother, are granted citizenship under the Law of Return, even though the Orthodox view them as gentiles.

Who would be the ringmaster if there were a binational state? Certainly neither the Orthodox nor Muslim establishments. No doubt, marginal accommodations could be made over religion for both Jews and Muslims, but the laws governing Israel-Palestine would inevitably be basically secular. A binational state would be a democracy governed by democratic institutions. There would be political parties representing Jews and Muslims, elections, a constitution, and so forth. Such a vision was potentially feasible at the beginning of the twentieth century, but now? It is too late. Israel will never allow it.

6.6 PETER sighs:

We sigh together, no doubt, Dan. A practical solution that satisfies demands of both Jews and Palestinians remains elusive. Mind you, that need not be the case. Many Jews and many Palestinians – Judaic, Islamic and neither – could get on perfectly well within a secular state; and some do here in the current Western versions of secularism. The problem is that Israel is not truly secular, whatever you say to the contrary, Dan. The Law of Return applies solely to Jews, however identified. Israel's latest incarnation is explicitly for the Jews.

It is true that the driving force behind modern Israel was David Ben-Gurion, who was no lover of Judaism; at times he seemed atheist – at others, pantheistic. As modern Israel's first leader, on the 14th of May, 1948, he put forward the Declaration of the Establishment of the State of Israel; it includes:

> The State of Israel will be open for Jewish immigration and for the Ingathering of the Exiles; it will foster the development of the country for the benefit of all its inhabitants; it will be based on freedom, justice and peace as envisaged by the prophets of Israel; it will ensure complete equality of social and political rights to all its inhabitants irrespective of religion, race or sex.

Whatever Ben-Gurion's noble intentions, can anyone rationally believe that today's Israel applies those ideals (or even aspires to apply those ideals) to the Palestinians? A similar question may be asked of our Western liberal states.

Modern Israel was instituted to give an exiled and suffering people – the Jews – an autonomous homeland. In doing so, it created suffering and exile for another people, the Palestinians, a catastrophe, the Nakba, as noted earlier. I do not thereby imply that Jewish Israel's intentions and actions are akin to Nazi Germany's intentions and actions, ones that led to the Holocaust, with its planned horrors, deaths and genocidal aim.

By the way, although 'Holocaust' is a common term for the Jewish tragedy (and we use it throughout in this work), the Hebrew 'Shoah' (calamity) is perhaps more apt. That is because 'Holocaust' has etymological links to sacrifice through burning.

Israel declares itself a democracy – proudly so, with good reason, in view of the surrounding Middle Eastern states. In a few generations' time, who knows how the majority in Israel will vote? That question arises even if Jews remain the majority; current generations cannot bind votes of future generations. How the majority may vote arises all the more pertinently, were Muslims to become Israel's majority – and have the vote. The resultant State Ringmaster would be unlikely to permit homosexual relations, women unveiled in public and satirical portrayals of Mohammad.

Why save the whale? – not this or that particular whale, but the species whale (I use the term 'species' loosely). Why be upset at the demise of the dodo? No, Dan, I am not losing the thread.

We save the whale not for the sake of the species – it has no sake – but either because we humans value having that mammalian variety around or because that species and species diversity possess intrinsic value. Perhaps 'a people' has intrinsic value just as – maybe even more than – does the whale. Many of us like and value having different peoples around. Sadly, some lack that like, that valuation – especially when it comes to the Jewish people, as we next discuss.

Mullings

Dan asks:
   Must the Jewish people continue to exist, not least to confound Hitler who insisted that they should have no posthumous victory?

Peter asks:
   Is preserving Jewishness in future generations nothing but Jewish vanity, all vanity?

Chapter Seven
Why are Jews so hated?

7.1 DAN writes:

In the Greco-Roman world, Jews were viewed as alien and xenophobic. In Hellenistic society the common view was that anything non-Greek was uncivilized. In this context, Judaism was regarded with contempt. With the emergence of Christianity such hostility towards Jewry intensified. Christianity absorbed pagan antipathy to the Jewish people and utilized aspects of Pharisaic Judaism to distance itself from the faith from which it had evolved. Such anti-Jewish sentiment became an essential element of Christianity.

The New Testament served as a basis for the early Church's vilification of the Jews. According to the Church Fathers, the Jewish people are lawless and dissolute. Because of their rejection of Jesus, the Jewish nation has been excluded from God's grace and is subject to his wrath. The Adversus Judaeos teaching of the early Church Fathers continued into the medieval period and beyond. Even though eighteenth-century champions of the Enlightenment sought to ameliorate the conditions under which Jews lived, others attacked Jews on the basis of misconceived rationalist and scientific assumptions. During the twentieth century, antagonism toward Jews continued unabated.

Such Judeophobia served as the background to the rise of Nazism. According to Hitler, Jews constituted a vile race intent on seizing control of political, social and economic affairs. As a result, the Jewish community was subjected to a series of restrictive measures and eventual plans for extermination. Throughout this period the Nazis sought to bring about the total destruction of the Jewish nation. In the post-Holocaust world, Jews became intent on protecting themselves in their ancestral homeland – in Palestine. However, contrary to Zionist aspirations, modern-day Israel has fuelled Arab hatred of Jewry.

7.2 PETER responds:

Your opening salvo, Dan, if salvo it be, outlines the historical continuity of antisemitism through ages and across nations. There is not, though, much by way of explanation of why Jews have been so distinctively hated.

Putting to one side the Nazis' obsessive hatred, are we right in thinking that hatred has been more widespread and deeper against Jews than against other groupings – cultures, nationalities, religions? If we are right, does that hatred focus on something distinctively Jewish? Or might it have been Jew-directed simply because Jews happened to be the distinctive 'others' then in view. Look at the US and Europe today: my guess is that Islamophobia is far greater than Judeophobia. Which 'others' receive the lion's share of hatred can depend on contingent matters, such as their proportionate numbers, their visibility, powers and perceived threats.

I could be wrong – of course, of course. Perhaps there is an essential difference between Islamophobia and Judeophobia. Islamophobia is hatred of Islam, a religion, an ideology, as interpreted in a certain way, whereas Judeophobia is, it seems – contrary to my musing above – a hatred of a people including those Jews with no commitment to Judaism. As said in the Prologue, we are using 'Judeophobia', 'Jew-hatred', 'antisemitism' as in practice amounting to the same unfortunate characteristic hatred. Could that hatred be aimed at Jews because they still value ancestors who identified with Judaism, with being the 'chosen people'? If one pupil at school is 'Teacher's Pet' it is not unusual for others, the non-pets, to gang up against that favoured one.

As you point out, Dan, a distinctive Jewish action that reaped continual negative coverage was the instigation of Jesus's death. Jesus, though, presumably was a Jew, at least by the mother's line. Even those who deny that Jesus was Jewish, and hence deny that the Jews instigated the death of one of their own, have to accept that subsequent Jews have not killed Jesus. With regard to other activities linked with Jews, Jews were once distinctive in their engagement in usury; early Christians and then Muslims condemned the practice. Today, though, Christians and many, many others embrace usury; even Muslims dance little investment waltzes to achieve the same usur-ian outcome.

The question is: what – if anything – do today's Jews get up to, or what characteristics do they possess, in virtue of which they receive extreme hatred? I bet that most people today who manifest Jew-hatred have little interest in what Jews did two thousand years ago.

7.3 DAN replies:

You ask about the nature of Jew-hatred. In the past, Jews were portrayed as having curly black hair, large hooked noses, and dark-coloured beady eyes. Jews were also frequently depicted as having red hair which was identified with the villain Judas Iscariot in the New Testament. During the Spanish Inquisition all those with red hair were identified as Jews, and writers from Shakespeare to Dickens identified Jewish characters by giving them red hair.

Golda Meir, Prime Minister (1969–1974)

"Even paranoids have real enemies."

Why such a depiction? As you know, Jews were historically regarded as Christ-killers and enemies of Christianity and Christendom. In this light, Jews were depicted as satanic cohorts or devils themselves. In modern times, the Nazis drew on such ancient stereotypic beliefs in the proclamation of the racial inferiority of Jews and their evil intentions.

In *Mein Kampf*, Hitler wrote:

> With satanic joy in his face, the black-haired Jewish youth lurks in wait for the unsuspecting girl whom he defiles with his blood, thus stealing her from her people. With every means he tries to destroy the racial foundations of the people he has set out to subjugate... It was and it is Jews who bring the Negroes into the Rhineland, always with the same secret thought and clear aim of ruining the hated white race by the necessarily resulting bastardization, throwing it down from its cultural and political height, and himself rising to be its master.

Of course, you are right that other groups have been persecuted throughout history. But it is undeniable that we have endured prejudice and contempt for a very long time. For nearly four millennia we have been detested. The twentieth century witnessed a policy of Jewish genocide that destroyed the lives of six million Jews. Such hatred is the background to understanding our history and our determination to survive. It is in this light that Israel must be seen as the key to the Jewish future. For the vast majority of Jews, it is the refuge in the storm.

7.4 PETER sighs:

You usefully tell me, Dan, that the Nazis deployed the image of Jews as racially inferior, satanic, possessed of evil intent; but why did they use that image? Did they sincerely believe it? Whatever the answers, why have others continued with Jew-hatred?

When, centuries ago, Christians saw Jews as Jesus-killers, we may understand the hatred. Well, we may understand, if we accept collective responsibility. Jesus, though, was Jewish; the direct killers of Jesus were Romans – yet hatred of Romans has not persisted. I draw a veil over Silvio Berlusconi; anyway, he was born in Milan.

Allow me to emphasize points already grazed. Jews are historically associated with profitable money lending, but there is no good reason to believe that today's antisemites deplore such lending. Where would capitalism be without it? I doubt if many antisemites know much about the Jewish role in Jesus's death; possibly some do – but do they maintain that alleged sins from two millennia ago merit today's antisemitism? Many Japanese and Germans, only a few decades ago, caused much suffering to, for example, the British and Americans, yet the typical Japanese and Germans of today are not reviled.

My Japanese/German analogy may miss the point. Those horrendous deeds were bounded by wartime. Further, most Germans do not identify with the Nazis; and Nazis are still usually reviled. By contrast, the Jews – atheist or religious – do identify themselves very much as Jewish, as a people with a unique history. Perhaps, then, it is unsurprising that non-Jews see Jews in that way, and hence may fall into holding the anti-Jew prejudices of previous generations.

Beliefs, attitudes, emotions are contagious; they can be difficult to dislodge, however inappropriate they have become. Yes, the image of Jews as miserly and wealthy, committed to 'money, money, money', persists, yet many non-Jews are miserly and wealthy, obsessed with money – and many, many Jews are poor, generous and charitable. Some antisemites apparently believe Jewish capitalists conspire to dominate the world, ignoring the many non-Jewish capitalists who could be viewed in a similar fashion – and forgetting the many Jews who have fought for international socialist principles.

In a few decades' time, will the West's spotlight of hatred be aimed at Muslims? That could easily become so, if Muslims are increasingly readily identified through distinctive garb, calls to prayer, religious superiority, and an insistence on separateness from others, courtesy of the veil. After all – Orthodox Jews apart – the distinctiveness of Jews may one day have paled into insignificance.

7.5 DAN argues further:

You are right that in Western countries previous forms of antisemitism have faded with time. The Church no longer castigates Jews as Christ-killers. Instead, a wide variety of interfaith organizations have been established to encourage Jewish-Christian encounters and foster religious understanding. Further, in Western countries, racial hostility toward Jews has vanished; racial theories about Jews have been completely discredited.

Yet the creation of a Jewish state in the Holy Land has fuelled a new form of antisemitism: modern Arab Jew-hatred. During the last fifty years, a vast quantity of antisemitic literature has been published in Muslim countries utilizing religious as well as racial motifs. Some of this literature, such as Hitler's *Mein Kampf*, Henry Ford's

International Jew, and the *Protocols of the Elders of Zion*, have been translated into Arabic and are widely available.

> **The neighbours**
>
> A rich Jewish banker, Greenstein, lived next door to John D. Rockefeller. Both had enormous estates. Gradually, Greenstein built up the same fleet of Rolls Royces as those owned by Rockefeller. He also developed the same landscaping, waterfalls, swimming pool, and so forth. That copycat behaviour increasingly irritated Rockefeller.
>
> One day, Rockefeller explodes. 'Greenstein,' he says, 'Are you trying to be my equal? Do you actually think you can be like me by copying everything that I own?'
>
> 'I am not your equal,' responds Greenstein. 'I am better than you!'
>
> 'And how do you make that out?' – Rockefeller is indignant.
>
> 'Because,' says Greenstein, 'I don't have a Jew living next to me.'

Other writings have continued with negative stereotypical images of the Jew. These depictions have been reinterpreted to express Arab antipathy towards Jews: repeatedly the Jew is portrayed as an evil force determined to corrupt and exploit the society in which he lives. In addition, Jews are presented as forming a global conspiracy intent on dominating world affairs. As a result of such perceptions, many fundamentalist Muslims are intent on carrying out a jihad against the Jewish community. This highlights the ongoing presence of Jew-hatred in contemporary society. As humanity's most persistent hatred, antisemitism continues to flourish in the modern world.

7.6 PETER concludes with little by way of conclusion:

We are both guilty of some intellectual laziness, Dan. We have not always been clear about the 'where', 'when'. To make the point by an obvious example, I take it that hatred of Jews is not rife in Israel but is rife amongst Hamas supporters. I imagine that some non-religious Israeli Jews are not exactly happy about the Orthodox Jews – some degree of Judeophobia there – though probably that does not reach the depths of hatred.

Turning to the West's Judeophobia, I doubt if religion is directly involved, but maybe it is the belief that Jews see themselves as separate and superior. Some Jews committed to Judaism may well see themselves in that way. Whether so or not, it does not really explain the existence and degree of antisemitism present.

Let us remember – sadly remember – that it is not unusual for members of one ethnic group to hate members of another. Years ago, when I taught (well, tried to teach) in a London school, there was – to say the least – no love lost between many West Indians and Asians. Today, violent disparagements between certain groups persist. Academic discussions of how doubtful are the criteria for races, nations and peoples hold no sway; that various ethnic groups in Britain, for example, suffer the same socially and economically often generates little bonding between those groups.

My guess is that Western non-Islamic antisemites see the distinctive 'other' as a threat; they attack Jews one day but could just as readily attack distinctive 'others', such as Muslims, another day.

The key difference between Islam and Judaism/Jewishness, so a quip goes, is that the former urges non-Muslims to see the light and follow Islam, whereas Jews have no great wish to turn non-Jews into Jews, religious or otherwise. Why, then, should Jews have a problem in living their lives outside Israel? Let us see.

> **Mullings**
>
> Dan asks:
>> Is antisemitism inevitable if Jews are a minority group?
>
> Peter asks:
>> A child is born of Jewish parents: whatever he does, is he bound to be a potential target of antisemitism?

Part Two
Israel: 'This land is our land'

Chapter Eight

Is there a future for Jews and Judaism outside of Israel?

8.1 DAN writes:

When Zionism emerged at the end of the nineteenth century, secular Zionists argued that Jews would never be secure in the countries where they resided. In 1897, at the first Zionist Congress, Max Nordau, a co-founder of the World Zionist Organization, spoke about the condition of Jewry. Wherever Jews lived in large numbers, he declared, they were subject to misery. Proponents of Jewish emancipation argued that if legal restrictions against Jews were lifted, this would result in the amelioration of Jewish deprivation. This happened in the West, yet human beings do not live by bread alone. The old forms of misery, he stressed, have been replaced by new ones. Antisemitism exists even in the most enlightened countries. In *The Jewish State*, published prior to the Congress, Theodor Herzl argued that his campaign for a Jewish homeland was not utopian theory: rather, the enterprise was a realistic proposal arising from Jewish oppression and persecution.

That is the background to whether Jews and Judaism can survive and flourish outside the Holy Land. The early Zionist ideal of a state where all Jews could live securely was an idealistic vision. But the reality is that although Israel has today become a focus of Jewish existence, more Jews live outside the Holy Land than within its borders. Israel is an inspiration for Jews, but it cannot alone carry the weight of Jewish existence. Further, it is clear that Herzl and others were mistaken in thinking that the creation of a Jewish commonwealth in Palestine would solve the problem of Jew-hatred. They underestimated the ferocity of Arab opposition to the Zionist programme. Arab hostility is as intense as ever. Indeed, the future of Jewry and Judaism may have become even less secure with the threat of a nuclear holocaust looming in the background. Israel has armed itself with nuclear weapons, but a future nuclear conflict remains a possibility. Could Jewry withstand a further holocaust?

8.2 PETER responds:

Dan, you provide a valuable background to the chapter's question; but the question is curious, even though of common type. It transpired, at some stage, that neither the dodo nor the British Empire nor the Soviet Union had much of a future. Things look bleak for giraffes, cheetahs and giant pandas – but for Jews and Judaism? Clearly, they have some future both within and without Israel. The question is: how long and secure is that future?

> **A mezuzah?**
>
> A Jewish dentist asks an Orthodox rabbi for a mezuzah (a box with prayers, normally fixed on a doorpost) for his Jaguar car. The Orthodox rabbi is outraged, 'You can't put a mezuzah on a car – but you could try the Conservative rabbi whose synagogue is nearby.'
>
> The dentist visits the Conservative rabbi. He is told that his 'mezuzah for a car' is utterly stupid – but he could try the Reform rabbi whose Temple is close by.
>
> Our dentist trots off and finally meets the Reform rabbi, 'May I have a mezuzah for my Jaguar?'
>
> The rabbi warms to him, telling him how he also has a Jaguar, a gift from his wife's parents. He asks what model the rich man has, how many miles to the gallon and so forth. The dentist is thrilled with this bonding and returns to his request for a mezuzah.
>
> 'A mezuzah, a mezuzah?' questions the Reform rabbi. 'What's a mezuzah?'

Consider Jews and Judaism 'without' Israel. My 'without' has a pertinent ambiguity between Jews and Judaism 'outside' of Israel and Jews and Judaism existing when there is no Israel. Whether Jews living in Europe, Russia and America are more likely to have a future as Jews, given Israel's existence, than if no Israel existed, is an empirical question: look at the evidence. My speculation is that they are more likely to have a future. Israel shines as a physical and political manifestation of Jewish identity, one that is essential to many Jews.

A Jewish dentist

'Ah, a Jaguar – if only it had a mezuzah!'

We are, though, ignoring distinctions. Could the Jews remain as a people, bound together, even if Judaism died out? Presumably, one day all Jews could be free-and-easy Reform Jews, even atheistic Jews, while valuing their ancestry and traditions. Would today's Hasidic Jews still be pleased that Jews continued to be, even though ignorant of Judaism? Do we think that believers in Judaism could exist, even if all Jews died out? Is that a conceptual impossibility?

Reflect on today's non-Israeli Jews. They will have Jewish children who will have Jewish children – and so forth. Through marriages to non-Jews, through fading interest in themselves as Jewish, perhaps through fear of antisemitism, in a few generations those individuals may not see themselves as Jews; it may not matter to them and may not even cross their minds. Is that one way in which you would see the Jews as without future?

8.3 DAN thinks further:

You raise a fundamental question about the preservation of Judaism and the continuation of the Jewish people. We Jews have resolved that we must continue as a people. That is the meaning of the exhortation: we must survive! In the shadow of the Holocaust, we are determined not to give Hitler a posthumous victory. The State of Israel is viewed as an ultimate insurance policy. But what exactly is being preserved?

In the past, Jews were united by a common heritage. In ancient times, we were a nation living alongside the Assyrians, Babylonians and Egyptians as well as other peoples. With the destruction of the Temple in 70 CE by the Romans, Judaism continued under the leadership of rabbinic sages in Israel and the diaspora. Through the centuries, Jewish people were united by belief and practice. From generation to generation, rabbinic sages interpreted the religious heritage, and their teachings in the Mishnah and Talmud, as well as Midrashim, served as the basis for study. Over time, new groups such as the Karaites, the Sabbateans, and the Hasidim emerged with their different traditions, yet the Jewish people were unified by a common religious heritage.

Today, however, this is no longer the case. With the destruction of the ghetto walls at the end of the eighteenth century and the subsequent emancipation of Jewry, Judaism fragmented into a variety of denominations with radically different orientations.

In the quest to ensure Jewish survival, what, then, is being preserved? For the strictly Orthodox, the answer is clear: the traditional Jewish way of life. But beyond the strictly Orthodox, this is not the case. There is no longer an overarching religious system that unites us as a people. Instead we are a fractious, dysfunctional family. Yet, there is unanimity about the necessity of Jewish survival. We are determined to preserve the Jewish faith, even if we cannot agree what it is. We are resolved to endure, but it is not clear what we hope to accomplish other than survival itself.

8.4 PETER tries for elucidation:

Well, Dan, you speak of 'we Jews' having resolved to continue as a people. I take it that you are referring to the vast majority of Jews, be they Orthodox, Reform, humanistic – be they those who don't really care, save that they recognize themselves as Jews, as part of 'family', even if dysfunctional. Now, let me pin you down.

Suppose Orthodox Judaism completely died out. There would still exist the offspring of Orthodox Jews. Would Reform Jews be pleased that Orthodoxy had vanished? Upset? Indifferent? I am asking: where lies the importance, for Jews, in Jews continuing? Orthodox Jews would doubtless be distressed at my supposed loss of Orthodoxy, but would they comfort themselves with the thought that at least descendants of Jews survive? Minimally, would it be comforting that their offspring's offspring exist, even if those offspring place no value on their Jewishness, and, generations later, had no idea of Jewishness?

I ask similar questions of Reform Jews, such as your good self, Dan. Suppose – bizarrely, perhaps – that over the next generations, all Jews became highly committed to Orthodoxy. 'At least there are still Jews,' would you sigh with some satisfaction?

Let us use King's College, Cambridge again – and my humble membership. For centuries, it was a small, highly privileged, exclusive college for Etonians: would those members of the past be pleased that King's still exists, even though its reputation is now left-wing, its provosts usually atheistic and its students mainly state-educated? The developments have been gradual, with the iconic King's Chapel ever in view. There exists the unity of a thread running through the developments. Is that thread sufficient, though, for members over the centuries identifying as 'one'?

King's is a mere five centuries or so old. Jews have Jerusalem as their focus – a city somewhat older, with vastly greater significance. Will Jews, the people, exist as Jews, so long as they see themselves as having that unique relationship, that thread, with Jerusalem? Should that significance be lost – should the heritage of Jerusalem cease to count for anything – would that be the end of Jewry and Judaism? Of course, those future individuals would have Jewish ancestors, but – to speak paradoxically – those future Jews would not be Jews. Would that matter?

8.5 DAN reflects:

You are right to press me about what ultimately matters about Jewish survival. Jews themselves would not know exactly what to say. It is a universal sentiment that the Jewish people must continue and that the Jewish way of life should in some respect flourish. But given the deep divisions within the Jewish community, there is no consensus about what exactly should persist. Nonetheless, it is a universal sentiment that the Jewish people should go on from generation to generation.

Even if there is no overarching framework that draws Jews together as a religious group, there is the heartfelt determination that survival is critical. It is not enough for there to be descendants of Jews who remember their Jewish ancestors. It is critical that these descendants see themselves as Jews and revere their ancient heritage.

For strictly Orthodox Jews more is required. In their view, Judaism as it has been practised through the centuries must continue to animate the Jewish nation. Non-Orthodox Jews do not share such a religious vision. Given the divisions that exist in the Jewish community, there is no coherent understanding of the role of the nation. Yet, there is a fervent conviction that the Jewish tradition should animate Jewish life.

We are a proud people. The idea that we could vanish and leave behind only descendants who would not consider themselves as Jews is unthinkable. We do not wish to pass away as other civilizations have. This would be the ultimate tragedy. It is in this light that you should understand the Jewish commitment to the State of Israel. Our history has demonstrated to us the fragility of Jewish existence. Since the loss of our ancient homeland in the first century, we have wandered as a minority people from country to country. Our neighbours hated and despised us. The Nazis attempted to annihilate us. For most Jews, Israel is a refuge in the storm, the only real hope of survival.

8.6 PETER concludes, with more questions:

Over these exchanges, dear Dan, you have made much use of the 'we': '*we* are a proud people'; '*our* contribution to the arts, sciences and culture'. I admire yet hesitate before such collective identity. Upon which characteristics does the 'we' rely? Using my King's membership again, have 'we' members made significant contributions? Well, no; some members have, radically so – the institution has – but a 'we' that includes me and all others?

Collective identity leads to collective responsibility. The Jews, two millennia ago, killed Jesus, it is said; so, today's Jews must be punished. Jewish Israel has mistreated Palestinians; so Israel should be boycotted, damaging many Israeli Jews, including protestors against Israeli policies. The Jewish 'we, the Jewish people' welcomes collective praise, but brings along the dangers of collective blame. Beware collective identity.

Consider the following: morality demands detachment from the personal when distributing justice, essay grades or shop service. I ought not to give Dan a high essay mark because he is a friend; of course, his being my friend ought not to inhibit my giving him a high mark, were he to deserve it – a logical possibility, I guess,

Dan. Morality, though, is not always detached in that way; it also warms to personal attachments: when you can save only one person from drowning – one is a stranger, the other is your daughter – 'Whom ought I to save?' is one question too many. Suppose, Dan, you can save only one of two strangers, but one is a Jew, the other gentile. Would you – ought you to – save the Jew because you both are Jews? Does Jewishness justify such attachment?

Consider: a teenage Lucinda knows that by age sixty, her beliefs, attitudes and memories may all have changed, yet she worries about that future. 'It will still be *me*.' There's continuity in the life, but she, as teenager, will not experience herself as the sixty-year old. Dan, you will not experience Jewish life in one hundred years' time, yet it matters to you – and matters, as a mysterious attachment 'as Jew'. That is, indeed, mysterious.

We value things existing after our demise – whales, walruses and the wilderness; the works of Plato, Picasso and Prokofiev. Those are detached valuations. Jews value Jews existing, yet also from an attached 'we Jews' perspective, akin to Lucinda's 'It will still be me'.

Jewish identity seems grounded in the value that Jews give to their identity persisting: a self-valuing 'circular' identity. Perhaps, though, the Jewish persistence is properly grounded

– literally grounded – in the attachment to Jerusalem. That returns us to the special relationship with a contested land – with peoples in conflict – as we next confront.

> **Mullings**
>
> Dan asks:
> If Jews have abandoned religious belief, is there any point in the survival of Judaism?
>
> Peter asks:
> Is there any greater value in Jews continuing to exist for another thousand years than the French, Germans and Palestinians – even than whales, rainforests and oceans?

Chapter Nine

What determines a nation's territorial rights?

9.1 DAN sets the scene:

The issue of territorial rights is easily settled where a particular nation has inhabited land for centuries. But there is a problem when two peoples have lived in the same territory at different periods. This is the case regarding Palestine which was the homeland for Jewry thousands of years ago, and in recent times was inhabited by Arabs. Whose land is it? The vast majority of Jews believe it belongs to them.

On the 29th November, 1947, the United Nations General Assembly passed a resolution calling for the establishment of a Jewish State in Eretz-Israel (land of Israel); the General Assembly required the inhabitants of Eretz-Israel to take such steps as were necessary on their part for the implementation of that resolution. According to Jewry, this recognition by the United Nations of the right of the Jewish people to establish their State is irrevocable.

Palestinians dispute such claims. In their view, Jews have no right to the land of Palestine. The history of Jewish Palestine ended in 137 CE, they maintain. Until the middle of the twentieth century, there had not been a Jewish majority in the country. As a consequence of illegitimate Zionist aspirations, there has been the dispersion and destruction of a settled, indigenous population.

But does the Holy Land belong to the Palestinians? Or does it belong to Jewry? There are two competing narratives about ownership. The Jewish position is based on ancient history and the age-old longing to return to the country that was theirs for over a millennium. The Arab's critique is grounded in the facts of more recent centuries of occupation. These competing arguments have tragically resulted in a century of bloodshed, and there seems no way to reconcile such conflicting aspirations. The Palestinian protest in May 2018 against the establishment of a US embassy in Jerusalem and the fierce Israeli retaliation highlight such seemingly irreconcilable viewpoints.

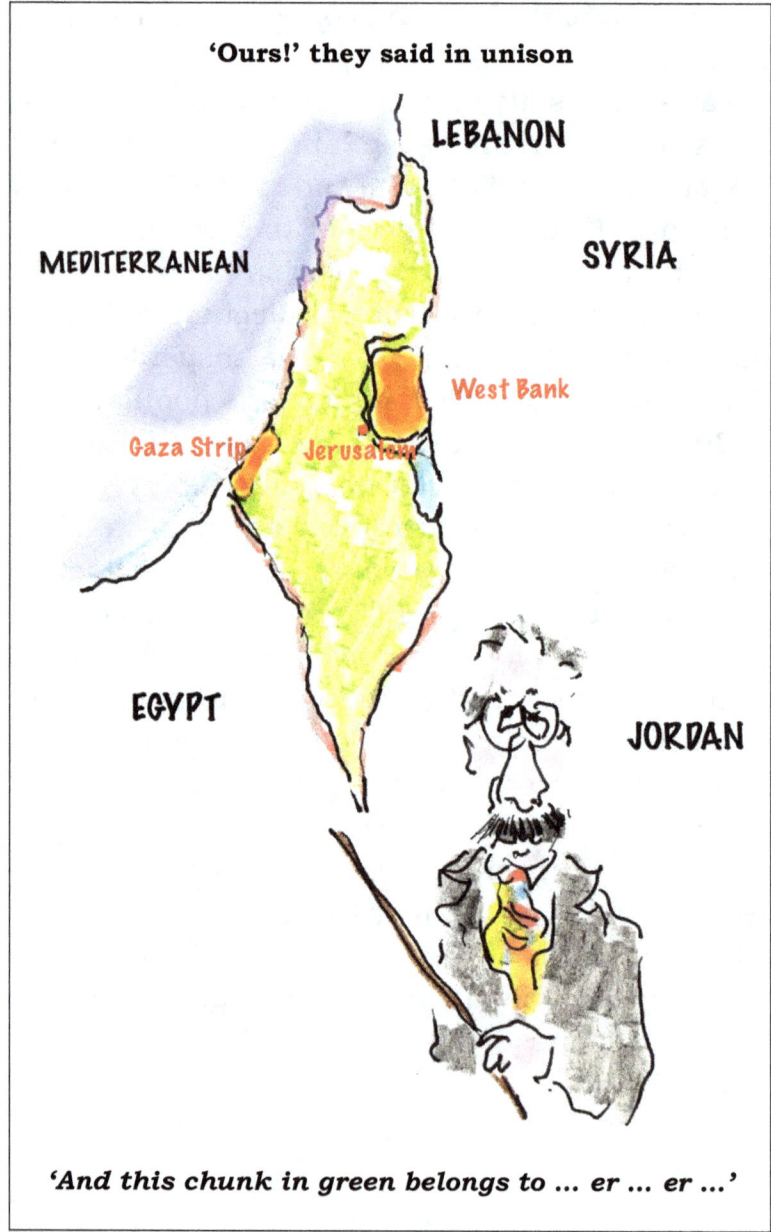

9.2 PETER responds:

Why think that any nation – community, individual – has rights over a parcel of land? That is a background worry that should unsettle us if tempted to accept your initial observation, Dan, that territorial rights are easily settled when only one nation has inhabited a land. The starting point could be that land ownership is no more justified than ownership of the air, oceans and sunsets; it could be that land belongs to all human beings – or, better, all creatures – or even belongs to God, on loan to all creatures.

Assume that there is good justification for people owning some territory: we may yet wonder whether any good justification exists for why ownership is of this portion rather than that. That wonderment returns us directly to the Palestinian-Israeli conflict. Should land ownership be on a 'first come; first served' basis? Should it be on the basis of how much has been invested in the land – infrastructure, homes, services – by current or former occupiers? Should it be founded on how significant the land is to that particular people's identity? Perhaps it should be a combination of those factors, with inevitable disputes about weightings and grey areas.

Realism – brute political reality, violence and force – trumps, it seems, concerns of fairness. Europeans, settling in North America, drove many natives from their homelands; there is no question of returning their land. Over the centuries, lands have been divided, passed from losers to victors and sometimes back again. In many cases, people have, generations later, sighed and accepted the outcome – but not yet over the Holy Land.

There currently is no international acceptance of Israel as a glorious and secure victor. Some Israeli Jews feel uneasy and guilty about how Israel's existence has led to despairing miseries of many Palestinians. Probably religion remains one major factor in the continuing Arab/Jew conflict. Am I right, I wonder, in thinking that Judaism has nothing much to say about the Palestinian misery created by the Jewish recapture of Jerusalem?

9.3 DAN mulls over Peter's view:

You write: 'The starting point could be that ownership of land can be no more justified than ownership of the air, oceans and sunsets; it could be that land belongs to all human beings.' This is a very odd view. Ownership of property is a legal matter. Determining who owns what – whether objects or land – involves rights and duties.

What determines a nation's territorial rights? 115

Property can be acquired in a wide variety of ways: it can be purchased with money, traded for other property, won in a bet, inherited, received as damages, exchanged for other property, received as a gift. Yet, no matter how it is obtained, it is protected by law. The point is that the legal system provides a framework for determining who owns what. Contrary to what you say, property does not belong equally to all human beings regardless of circumstances.

Let me return to the arguments deployed by Jewry. In the view of the Zionists, the Holy Land was promised to the Jewish people by God, and subsequently conquered thousands of years ago by the ancient Israelites and inhabited for over a thousand years. Palestinians, however, maintain that the Zionists in the nineteenth and twentieth centuries were usurpers of their land. The vast majority of those living in Palestine prior to massive immigration in the twentieth century were Arabs who had inhabited the country for centuries.

In the Arab view, the early Zionists had no right to settle in a country which was not legitimately theirs. Nor had the British the right to issue the Balfour Declaration which legitimized the Jewish usurpation of land which did not belong to them. Nor, finally, did the United Nations have the right to assign land to both Jews and Palestinians.

Despite this clash of views between Jews and Palestinians, it does not mean that Jews cannot empathize with Palestinian suffering.

9.4 PETER leads into controversy:

I am to blame for questioning the 'ownership' of land. To be told, though, that it is a legal matter, Dan, is of no help; the law may be based on error or immorality. Hitler's laws legitimated horrendous treatments of the Jews and confiscation of their property; that legality was no good justification for the treatment.

Numerous people discuss how to judge the rightful ownership of the Holy Land, even though the United Nations' assignment made Israel's ownership of some parts internationally legal. Legality is no secure indicator of what is morally right. We look for something morally to justify the Jewish ownership. You point to the history and significance for the Jews of the Holy Land; others, in opposition, point to similar factors for the Palestinians.

My body, we may argue, is properly mine, proper to me; it is my property, if anything is. That forms a starting point, one found in John Locke's political writings of the seventeenth century, for arguing that my labour is properly mine and what I work on – including the land – becomes properly mine. That line of argument, a somewhat dubious line, can lead Jews to justify claiming Jerusalem as properly theirs; it is an extension of the Jewish people's body. Of course, the Palestinians may attempt a similar justification.

Property rights, though, do not exhaust morality. Even if the Holy Land justly belongs to the Jews, has not Jewish insistence on territorial rights left others destitute, without good lands of their own? Have not the Palestinians been degraded and effectively imprisoned in Gaza and the West Bank?

Regarding the Palestinian plight, should the focus be solely on Israel's actions? Let us think on. Various Arab nations eagerly voice their support for their Palestinian 'brothers'. They have gone to war in support of the Palestinians. Mind you, at one stage the Jordanians annexed the Palestinian West Bank; so, maybe all is not brotherly love. Still, the Arab lands are vast compared with Israel's. Ought not we to wonder why those Arab nations have not shown compassion by providing the Palestinians with a land of their own?

Let us remember: Israelis have a reason not to yield much to the Palestinians; current Palestinian leaderships speak of driving the Jews from the

Middle East. By contrast, the Palestinians pose no existential threat to their Arab neighbours.

9.5 DAN reacts:

You consider the suggestion that Arab countries should have provided a home for the indigenous Arab population of Palestine. This was the view of Revisionist Zionists, early in the twentieth century. At that time the region covered by the British Mandate for Palestine included the modern-

Whose land?

'Well, don't ask me!'

day territories of Israel, the West Bank, Gaza and Jordan. Revisionist Zionists, led by Vladimir Jabotinsky, believed that the Jews should be given this territory and that most Palestinian Arabs could live in other Arab lands.

In 1937, Jabotinsky gave evidence before the Royal Commission on Palestine. Such a solution, he argued, would not be

> a hardship on any race, any nation, possessing so many national states now and so many more national states in the future. One fraction, one branch of that race, and not a big one, will have to live in someone else's state.

His point was that the Palestinians have plenty of Arab states where they could live. The Jews need Israel in order to have just one. For over one hundred years this has been the argument of right-wing Zionists. Yet, is it morally acceptable to compel an indigenous population to vacate their homes and lands which they have possessed for centuries because of the needs of another nation? Is this not theft and usurpation?

In the eyes of Palestinians and their supporters, such a dislocation of an indigenous population is a moral outrage. In *The Palestine-Israeli Conflict*, Dawoud El-Alami, a Muslim academic, bitterly complains about the Zionist enterprise:

> By definition the creation of a state based on religion and ethnicity in an inhabited land can only be achieved

by a degree of ethnic cleansing. The state built by a people who have long been victims institutionalizes a form of ethnic and religious disorientation that would not be acceptable in any other modern state.

This is a disturbing critique, and it calls into question the idea that Palestinians should be satisfied with land in other Arab countries as Jabotinsky suggests and perhaps you were supporting.

9.6 PETER concludes, bleakly so:

Allow me to address Dawoud El-Alami's heart-felt criticism – sorry, 'critique' – of Israel's existence.
    One objection is to Israel's discrimination in favour of Jews. I should respect those who raise that objection, were they as vocal against similar discriminations in Islamic states – states that are radically less tolerant than Israel. El-Alami opposes Israel's 'ethnic cleansing'. I should respect that opposition more were the voices of opposition just as vocal against, for example, Nazi Germany, ethnic displacements in South Sudan and mistreatments of minorities in Sri Lanka and Myanmar.

What determines a nation's territorial rights? 121

> **'Impossible?' you say**
>
> Harold Goldberg and Seth Horowitz were business partners. They couldn't agree about policy, so they decided to go to the rabbi for his opinion.
>
> Harold went first. When he finished, the rabbi stroked his beard and said, 'You're right.'
>
> Seth then presented his argument. When he finished, the rabbi nodded his head and said: 'You're right.'
>
> 'Wait a minute,' Harold said. 'We can't both be right.'
>
> 'You're right,' said the rabbi.

I am not arguing that, because discriminations and cleansings exist worldwide, we may ignore Israeli ones. I am arguing that many (though not all) objectors to Israel manifest little concern about similar outrages. I am tempted to ask: why pick on the Jews?

Regarding rightful territorial ownership, we muddle through. During the nineteenth century and early twentieth, some Palestinian land was purchased by Jewish funds with Zionist aspirations, but that no more justified Jewish political control than recent Russian investment in expensive London properties justifies Russians running London. There is, of course, no Godlike answer, though were we to believe in such, the Jews could uniquely claim Jerusalem as their promised land. Perhaps – *perhaps* – there is, though, more value in encouraging the thought 'I happen to be here' instead of the thought 'This is mine'.

Israelis and Palestinians – more, widely, Arabs; wider still, Americans and Europeans – need, I impotently suggest, to demote 'rights' considerations over who owns what. Focus, instead, on virtues: compassion, benevolence, generosity. Let wealthy Middle Eastern nations improve the lot of Palestinians by offering prosperous settlements in their lands, instead of urging revenge on the Jews. Let wealthy American Jews offer help to Palestinians, encouraging trade and reconciliation. Of course, that is easy to say – and two fundamental questions remain.

First, is it morally acceptable for states to prefer one religion, one ethnicity, over others? Today's Western anti-discrimination ethos greatly opposes such discrimination. My inclination is to oppose, except... Well, I value, in John Stuart Mill's expression – Mill, the great Victorian thinker, author of *On Liberty* – 'experiments in living'. I cannot see why that liberal attitude should not apply to states. Diversity of nations has value; it would be lost, if all nations were to sing from the same non-discriminatory non-religious hymn sheet. As a minor example, the diversity of colourful European currencies – with frustrations and excitements of exchanging Francs, Deutsche

What determines a nation's territorial rights? 123

Marks and Lira – has been lost. That move into conformity strikes me as, indeed, a loss.

Secondly, why do Palestinians and Israelis assume that their peoples will not change? Further, their future generations have not yet stepped into the Middle East; so, whatever justifies 'this land' as their homeland? No doubt many will believe it to be so, but only because, from birth, they will have been told so – dare we say, 'indoctrinated' so? They will have had 'collective identity' dinned into them – and that has major problems, as we see next.

Mullings

Dan asks:
  Should Palestinians be content to live fruitful lives in Arab countries? Or must they have their own nation state?

Peter asks:
  Even if 'this land' is ours *now*, why think that it must therefore belong to our future generations?

Chapter Ten

Are Jews collectively responsible for Israeli military actions?

10.1 DAN writes:

It makes no sense to blame the Jewish people for the actions of Israel. Jews living in the diaspora have no influence on Israeli policy. It is important to remember that Israel is a democracy, and that Israeli society is deeply divided politically. In Israel itself these various factions press for dramatically different solutions to the Israeli-Palestinian conflict. Consequently, given the political divide that exists in Israel, it would be a fundamental error to criminalize all Jews for the actions of the current Israeli government.

There are in fact many Jews worldwide who are bitterly critical of Israel's actions in recent years. A typical example of such opposition is the organization *Jews for Justice for Palestinians*. This is their creed:

WE BELIEVE THAT

- Lasting peace between Israel and the Palestinians requires justice, mutual recognition and respect.
- Peace requires ending Israel's illegal occupation and settlement of Palestinian land, including its illegal blockade of Gaza.
- Peace requires Israel to acknowledge its responsibility in the creation of the Palestinian refugees, and its obligation to negotiate a just, fair and practical resolution of the issue.
- Violence against civilians, no matter who commits it, is unacceptable.
- Israel's repressive policies in the West Bank and Gaza are breeding hatred and resentment.
- Israel's discrimination against its Palestinian citizens is unacceptable.
- It is crucial that Jews speak out for Palestinians' human rights.
- The humanitarian values of Judaism have been corrupted by the Israeli state's abuses of human rights.
- Britain, the EU, the USA, Russia and the UN must be persuaded to implement UN resolutions on Palestine.

The point is that 'world Jewry' does not speak with one voice. Both in the diaspora and Israel itself there are deep divisions. When Arabs and others attack Jews for their dedication to Israel, they fail to recognize that the Jewish community is not monolithic. Instead, political opinions range across a wide spectrum. The vast majority of Jews fully endorse the existence of a Jewish state in the Holy Land, but it is a mistake to think that there is universal support for the policies of the Netanyahu government.

10.2 PETER responds:

Dear Dan, you are wrong – of course – to say that it makes 'no sense' to blame the Jewish people for Israeli actions. It makes sense but is morally mistaken. Or is it? Consider examples of accepted collective responsibility – well, collective responsibility in some sense.

Recently, Britain apologized for its treatment of homosexuals decades ago. Britain offered sincere regrets for its torture of Kenyans in the 1950s. Maybe no British citizen alive at the time of the government's apologizing and regretting had been involved in any of the mistreatings – yet, Britain as a collective felt responsible for its past actions. In the Kenyan case, Britain paid compensation which came from current taxpayers with nothing to do with the torture.

Some traditions place importance on the family. There are instances where, because, say, a son of Family X has dishonoured the daughter of Family Y by raping her, Family Y demands the right to impose something equivalent, as punishment, on a daughter of Family X. That is an unpleasant family version of collective responsibility.

Controversially, I should liken that dishonouring family case to the stance held by many that a family's children 'deserve' to inherit from their parents. That stance leads many to oppose inheritance tax, estate duties, so-called death taxes. 'The family' is considered a unit – when it suits people. To tax money moving from the deceased parents' estate to the offspring is seen as unjust as taxing money if moving it from one's right pocket to one's left.

Those examples show that collective identity and responsibility, whether justified or not, is upheld in various relationships. Now, the Jews see themselves as 'a people' *par excellence*, so, perhaps they cannot easily wash their hands of activities engaged by prominent members. After all, the Holocaust sufferings gave an impetus to the existence of modern Israel which benefits later Jews; they deserve those benefits, it is argued, because all are of that Jewish collective identity. Highlighting one's identity, supporting the existence of Israel, sits uneasily with insisting – when the going gets tough – that one has no responsibility for what Jewish Israel does, when disagreeing with what it does.

10.3 DAN strongly disagrees:

It is true that the United Kingdom has offered sincere regrets for the way in which Kenyans were tortured. Britain has also apologized for the way homosexuals were treated. Some families have been held culpable for the ways family members have been treated. In these cases, there is collective responsibility. If you were referring to the need for the State of Israel to express remorse and offer apologies for the ways in which Palestinians have been treated, you suggest this would be a parallel case.

Yet, most Jews do not live in Israel. Why should they be held responsible for Israeli policy if they have no voice in determining what it is? Diaspora Jews such as I have no role in Israeli society. We have the right to immigrate, but if we have not done so, then we are under no obligation to offer apologies on behalf of a nation where we are not citizens. Why, for example, should those of French background living in Britain apologize for French policy?

> **The Deli**
>
> A Jewish deli guy sees an Arab walk in, an obvious sheikh, complete with robe and headdress. The Arab asks for twenty corned beef sandwiches; the deli guy whispers to his boss, 'There's an Arab who wants twenty corned beef sandwiches. What should I do?' His boss quickly responds, 'Tell him they're twenty bucks apiece.' The counter guy makes the sandwiches, and the Arab pays up with no argument.
>
> The next day the Arab returns and asks for sixty corned beef sandwiches. The counter guy whispers to his boss, who says, 'Tell him they cost sixty bucks each.' Again, all goes well; the Arab pays without question.
>
> The next day a similar thing happens: the Arab asks for and receives a hundred corned beef sandwiches at a hundred dollars each.
>
> The following day a sign goes up at the deli:
>
> **NO JEWS ALLOWED**

You say that one's identity as a Jew sits uneasily with denying responsibility for the action of other Jews, particularly in Israel. Here I think you are profoundly mistaken. The fact that I am Jewish does not obligate me to apologize to victims who have suffered at the hands of other Jews. I am embarrassed by their actions. But I am not culpable for what they have done. If Israel acts in ways that I oppose, I can object. I can lobby the Israeli government. I can feel sympathy for those who have suffered because of Israeli policy. But it is illogical for me as a diaspora Jew to feel obliged to apologize on behalf of a nation of which I have no part and whose actions I cannot directly affect.

10.4 PETER corrects:

Dan, dare I say, 'Pay attention!' Regarding my collective responsibility examples, I expressly said that I introduced them to make the point that 'collective responsibility', *whether justified or not*, is upheld in various relationships. If you want some opinions – I digress – estate duty, inheritance tax, strikes me as highly justified, yet the British government's apologies for actions decades ago, silly, unless read as emphasizing Britain's current rejection of such mistreatments. Now, regarding Jews' collective responsibility for Israel's actions, it is true that I wanted you to reflect, rather than simply wash your hands.

You rely heavily on the distinction between Israeli 'inside' Jews and diaspora Jews 'outside'. Only the former have a democratic influence on Israeli policies. How valuable, though, is that distinction, Dan? Consider Israeli Jews who oppose government policies: are they let off the responsibility hook for their government's actions? You may answer, 'No' because they engaged in voting. I may respond by saying diaspora Jews are, then, also hooked on the collective responsibility peg because they identify with Israel as essential to their Jewishness.

Interestingly, you recognize that you are sometimes *embarrassed* by the actions of Jews. Presumably those actions result from some features that you regard as typical Jewish, or are seen as such, even though you may lack those features or do not engage in such actions. As an American, although you did not vote for him, perhaps you are embarrassed by President Trump because he has some typical American characteristics.

Pride gives rise to similar 'identity' presuppositions. You are proud of Jewish intellectual contributions; presumably that pride is only appropriate if you feel that they derive, in part, from Jewishness with which you identify. Our embarrassment, shame or pride in others' activities requires linkages to us – otherwise why should we have such emotions? How tight might those links be? Should we, humanly linked, ashamed of the human capacity for war and selfishness?

Dan, you are embarrassed by Israel's anti-Palestinian actions, but (I assume) not by Chinese actions in Tibet. Why? Are you ashamed of Jewish Israeli actions because you are a Jew – or Zionist? Whichever it is, that you identify with a collective – in this case, the Jewish or Zionist community – clearly relates you emotionally to that collective's doings. Perhaps there should be collective shame, collective guilt, over bad things that get done, even if you play what I quip as 'the Egyptian card': namely, you remain in 'de-nial' of collective responsibility.

10.5 DAN responds:

I accept that you said 'whether justified or not' when discussing examples of collective responsibility. But the thrust of your argument is that there is in fact such a thing as 'collective responsibility', and that individuals have a moral duty to recognize such obligations. In particular, I thought you were pressing the case for all Jews to feel some responsibility for Israeli policy. If this is what you are saying, then I disagree.

Are Jews collectively responsible for Israeli attacks? 133

Washing those hands

'My hands were clean all along.'

The Israeli government is certainly responsible for its actions. It therefore has a duty to those who are affected by its policies. I would argue that in recent years, Israel has caused undue suffering to Palestinians. Some years ago, I wrote an article in the *Western Mail* (the main newspaper in Wales) in which I criticized Israel for bombing Gaza. Such a massive attack, I believed, was unjustified since it was disproportionate. The devastation brought about was excessive in relation to the destruction caused by rockets being fired into Israel. So, as a Jew, I should be concerned about Israeli politics, and it is right for me to criticize Israel when necessary. But, since I live in Britain, I do not feel any collective responsibility for its actions.

It is true that we Jews feel bound to one another. We are an ethnic community, tied together by tradition and history. It is for this reason that we are embarrassed when Jews such as Bernard Madoff act callously with no concern for others, when engaged in financial fraud. We deplore their immorality, and hope that such actions will not encourage antisemitism. Similarly, when Palestinians suffer terrible hardship, many Jews (whether they live in Israel or the diaspora) are deeply concerned about their welfare. But it is the Israeli government which must take responsibility, not individual Jews simply because they are Jewish. Conversely, Jews are proud of the achievements of other Jews, but they can take no credit for their accomplishments.

10.6 PETER muses on Dan's 'in denial':

You resist any collective responsibility, however small, for Israeli actions, even though you identify with the Jewish community and the fundamental importance of Israel to that community. That could be Dan in denial. I am not sure. I am sure, though, that it is no 'black or white' matter.

Some Israeli government ministers no doubt voted against government policies yet accepted collective responsibility. They freely accepted government posts; they did not resign. True, you did not freely become a Jew, but found yourself one; true, it is not easy to resign from Jewishness. In opposing Israeli policies, you distanced yourself 'as a Jew' – recognizing, it seems, your closer proximity to the policies than any gentiles' proximity.

Some Israeli voters strongly protest against the government's Palestinian policies. I am not clear if you see them, because they are Israeli, as having some collective responsibility, despite their protests. You also accept that the British government rightfully apologized for earlier mistreatments by the British, even though that government had nothing to do with them.

Those considerations show that there are no easy criteria for collective responsibility. Obviously, you had no causal role in Israeli policies; but does your strong identification with 'we Jews', specially attached to Israel, carry no burden of responsibility or guilt at all? Why does your Jewish identification generate shame without responsibility or guilt? I apologize for these questions, Dan. Obviously, I pose them to coax you into more reflection and perhaps acceptance of some (small) engagement with collective responsibility.

Imagine a close family – except that Sol, the son, goes off the rails. It is not the parents' fault, yet they accept responsibility for Sol's misdemeanors and pay for the damages he caused. 'They're just helping the victim and helping Sol out of a sticky position,' you may insist. 'They don't really think that they caused Sol to do what he did.' That may well be so, yet perhaps the light to cast on the situation is the following: as a family, they take on that responsibility, that guilt. Maybe that mildly links with the Christian idea of Jesus atoning for our sins – though I speak pretty much in ignorance over quite what that involves.

Even if there is no way in which numerous Jews can rightly be held causally responsible for Israel's actions, they may rightly feel ashamed and choose to carry the burden of collective responsibility and guilt. The bindings of a community cannot just be tightened and loosened by a member as best suits him – for that is not what it is to be a member of a community.

Mullings

Dan asks:
   Do we have any responsibility for actions done by others?

Peter asks:
   Can Jews wash their hands of Israel's actions as and when it makes for an easy life for them?

Chapter Eleven

One state, two states or no-state-at-all solution – and where?

11.1 DAN writes:

Before we discuss which alternative is best, we need to review the four possible scenarios for Jews and Palestinians living in the Holy Land:

(a) A Palestinian State: From the beginning of the Zionist movement, the indigenous Arab population was intent on driving out the Jewish inhabitants and curtailing any plans for a Jewish state in their midst. From the outset, the Arabs mounted an armed struggle, and this later materialized into a series of wars. The aim was to liberate Palestine from what was perceived as Jewish colonialism.

(b) A Jewish State: Throughout the history of Israel, there has never been a quest to drive all Palestinian Arabs from Israel. Instead, Arab inhabitants have been absorbed into the state and are regarded as full citizens. However, if a policy of ethnic cleansing were to take place accompanied by the annexation of the West Bank and Gaza, then there could be a mirror image of the first scenario with an exclusively Jewish population.

(c) A United-Palestine-Israel: Some early Zionists endorsed such a scheme, but this was a small minority. This is the third form of a One-State solution. There is very little enthusiasm today for such an idea in Jewish circles for fear that Israel would be overwhelmed by Palestinian refugees and others.

(d) Two States: Despite critics who maintain that the notion of a Two-State solution is dead, this seems today's most viable option, and it is being actively pursued by the Palestinian Authority. In 2011, Mahmoud Abbas submitted an application for the admission of Palestine to the United Nations on the basis of the 4 June 1967 borders. In his speech to the General Assembly on 23 September 2011, he applied for his people to be given the right to be called citizens of their own state. The Jewish community, however, is divided about such a proposal – some Jews believe it to be the only way forward; others are determined to curtail all efforts to create a Palestinian state alongside Israel.

These, then, are the alternatives which we need to consider. Which solution would be most viable and meet the needs of both Israelis and Palestinians?

11.2 PETER initiates a little controversy:

You ask, Dan, which of four possibilities would meet the needs of both Israelis and Palestinians. It may, though, be as impossible to satisfy their needs as to square the circle or construct a five-sided triangle in Euclidean space. In contrast to geometrical figures, people and peoples change.

Can the historical ties of one group to the Holy Land be shown to be weaker than another group's – or at least be weakened, in some way, for the better? Jewish ties would seem to have greater vital significance than Palestinian. If culture and ethnicity are to the fore, then the Palestinians could fit into other parts of the Middle East far more easily than could Jews, given the current ethos. If religion is to the fore, then the predominance of Islam amongst the Palestinians suggests that Palestinians would feel 'at home' in other Middle Eastern regions far more easily than could Jews.

Turn to 'weakening' the ties. 'Welcoming arms' from other Arab states, with land, safety and significant resources provided to the Palestinians, could well weaken Palestinian resolve to stay in the contested lands. No doubt, there would be initial refusals – 'we have lived here for generations' – but reflection on how much better the Palestinian lives of their children and grandchildren would be, secure in an Arab land, could tip the balance in favour of gradual moves. Of course, the suggestion requires benevolence and fellow-feeling by Arab brothers towards the Palestinians.

The suggestion may have the appearance of bribery, but that need not be the reality. If the transactions are voluntary – with compensations and benefits of relocation great – then it is no worse than (probably, it is more benign than) deals that often take place in countries, such as compulsory purchase of homes to make way for motorways.

Regarding my suggestion, Palestinians who decline relocation would be free to stay where they are, in Gaza for example, or even apply to Israel for citizenship; but, assuming many would take up the offer, pressures on Gaza, the West

Bank and Israel would reduce, perhaps leading to fresh ways of looking at relationships. Of course, 'pies and skies' may come to mind.

You never know

An Arab is nearly dying of thirst, crossing the desert, when he meets a Jew who, there in the middle of the desert, is selling ties. The Arab is furious for the Jew is urging him to buy a tie.

'Can't you see I'm dying of thirst?' the Arab screams, 'You lower-than-a-rat Jew – have you no mercy?'

The tie-selling Jew takes this on board. He tells the Arab that a few miles ahead, there is an air-conditioned restaurant where the Arab can get all the water he needs.

The Arab crawls painfully and slowly, making it over the sand dunes and vanishes – only to return hours later, gasping and obviously about to die.

'What has happened?' asks the Jew.

The Arab's last words are barely audible.

'They wouldn't let me in without a tie.'

11.3 DAN disagrees:

I think you underestimate the feelings of Jews and Palestinians about the Holy Land. For both peoples, it has profound religious significance. The suggestions you make about absorbing the Palestinians in the Arab world are unworkable. Neither the Arab states, nor the Palestinian people, wish for this to happen. Instead, the Arab world wishes that their Muslim brothers and sisters be settled in their ancient homeland, and this is the fervent wish of the Palestinians themselves.

The Arab's last words are barely audible. 'They wouldn't let me in without a tie.'

The only solution to the Palestine-Israeli conflict is the creation of a Palestinian state with Jerusalem as a capital for both peoples. This is the Two-State solution. In 2009, President Barack Obama spoke in Cairo about the necessity of creating a home for the Palestinians. There are, he said, two peoples with legitimate aspirations, each with a painful history that makes compromise elusive. It is easy to point fingers: for Palestinians to point to the displacement brought by Israel's founding, and for Israelis to point to the constant hostility and attacks throughout its history from within its borders as well as beyond. But, he continued, if we see this conflict only from one side or the other, then we will be blind to the truth: the only resolution is for the aspirations of both sides to be met through two states.

This is the only way forward. There can be no hope for peace while the Palestinians remain deprived of any recognized political identity. Now that we have a state of our own, we Jews should support the idea of a Two-State solution and UN recognition of Palestinian statehood. This, of course, will mean that a wide variety of issues will have to be faced for such an idea to become a reality. Yet, our past sufferings should bring us to understanding and compassion and the desire to relieve the suffering of others.

11.4 PETER responds:

You may well be right, Dan, that I underestimate the importance of the Holy Land for the Palestinians. My proposal, though, was not offered as an 'ideal' solution for, currently, there is no ideal. My proposal is two-fold.

First, Jerusalem to the Jews would seem to have more significance for them than to the Palestinians as Muslims. Jerusalem, according to Jewish belief, is the one place where God made them the 'chosen people'. True, that sounds bizarre, but it has a vitality, as myth or reality, for Jews. Palestinians as Muslims, I take it (maybe wrongly?), do not see themselves as the chosen people; further, they have more important religious sites, notably, Mecca.

The above suggests that, on grounds of religious significance, the prize of control of Jerusalem goes to the Jews. Of course, the Jews currently in Israel have less claim than the Palestinians regarding immediate ancestors having lived in that region; but presumably religious significance trumps proximity of ancestral location.

Secondly, my proposal contained no compulsion, but the offer to the Palestinians of flourishing lives, carrying into future generations. Many Arabs would no doubt urge the Palestinians to reject such offers; indeed, currently the Arabs would make no offers to help the Palestinians in the ways that I suggest. Would, though, poor Palestinian families, suffering the Gaza and West Bank plights, prefer to remain where they are over having radically better lives elsewhere?

Neither side of this tragic conflict, though, seems able to show much compassion and understanding for the other side; matters, as said earlier, are not helped when stress is on international legality and rights. Matters also are not helped when there is such disparity in power between Israel and Palestinian Gaza and the West Bank. Both our approaches, Dan, depend on compassion and understanding. That is why we shall both, no doubt, be disappointed.

A curiosity, already mentioned by me, is how both Jews and Palestinians claim to know what must morally be available to their descendants not yet born. Why impose that tradition on those future unknowns, hence, perpetuating conflicts? Are both Jews and Palestinians so convinced that their traditions must continue in the Holy Land, so proud, so determined, so self-indulgent, that they are prepared to pass on conflict, violence and outrage to future generations of Jews and Palestinians?

11.5 DAN responds:

You certainly have not underestimated the importance of Jerusalem for Jews, but I don't think you comprehend how important the city is to Muslims. Let me summarize both the Jewish and Islamic views. The Jewish connection to Jerusalem is ancient and powerful. Judaism made Jerusalem a holy city over three thousand years ago, and through all this time Jews have remained steadfast to it. Jews pray in its direction and mention its name constantly in their prayers and daily life.

The Passover service concludes with the prayer: Next year in Jerusalem! The destruction of the Temple looms large in Jewish consciousness. Its remembrance takes such forms as a special day of mourning, houses left partially unfinished, jewellery left incomplete, and a glass smashed during the wedding ceremony.

Whose?

'Mine!'

For Muslims, Jerusalem is also of fundamental importance. The Al-Aqsa Mosque is the third holiest site in Sunni Islam, after the mosques of Al-Haram in Mecca and Al-Nabawi in Medina. According to tradition, it was the first direction of prayer in Muhammad's lifetime, before the Ka'bah in Mecca. According to the Qur'an, Muhammad was taken by the miraculous steed to visit the farthest mosque which is identified with the Al-Aqsa Mosque in Jerusalem where he prayed and was then taken to the heavens in a single night in 620 CE. This event is known as Al-Isra'wal-Mi'raj (الإسراء والمعراج), 'The Night-Journey and the Ascension'.

It is not surprising, therefore, that there is bitter conflict about Jerusalem's status in both faiths. Jews today are insistent that it is the capital of Israel; Palestinians similarly contend that it must be the capital of Palestine. As I stated previously, I believe the aspirations of Jews and Palestinians must be reconciled. Hundreds of thousands of Palestinians live there, as do Jews. It will be a difficult task for negotiators to find a way forward, but they can and must if there is to be peace in the Holy Land.

11.6 PETER concludes – with realism and idealism:

Dan, you emphasize how critical it is to Palestinians to have 'their land' returned. I am unclear whether that is because they are Palestinians or because they are Muslims – or both. We zigzag between the two characterizations.

In simple arithmetical mode, if Islam is key, then Jerusalem is third on the list of significance for Muslims, whereas Jerusalem is the one and only hugely significant location for Jews. Muslims could recognize that difference – with a sense of generosity. If Jerusalem remains under Jewish authority, Islam still has complete control over two sites of greater significance.

Asymmetries are also relevant. With Jerusalem under Jewish authority, Muslims are permitted to visit their holy sites; when under Arab Jordanian authority, Jews were prohibited from their holy sites. Further, many Palestinians – maybe their leaderships are to blame – want to eradicate Israel; the Israelis seek no eradication of Palestinians.

Instead of emphasizing how critical Jerusalem is to Palestinian identity, perhaps the international community should be emphasizing how Palestinian lives deserve much better. Arab nations and Israel, together with the United States and Britain, need to be funding major reconstruction programmes in the Palestinian areas. Israel needs to take risks (again) by relaxing restrictions on Palestinian movements. Perhaps, as mentioned earlier, generous resettlement terms could be offered to Palestinians so that some may opt for new lives in other Arab states or the United States or Europe. Those measures may help a little to reduce the weight of the conflicting claims over the Holy Land.

Dan, you speak of reconciliation between Jews and Palestinians, but how can that arise if – *if* – the message is sent down the generations that all is woe until 'we' have exclusive ownership of Jerusalem and its surrounds? Which 'we' of course depends on which side is messaging. I return to 'generational change'. Who can tell what the great, great grandchildren of the Jewish Israelis and those of the Palestinians will think and want, if not so indoctrinated? Perhaps traditional Judaism and Islam will 'wither on the vine'? Perhaps future generations will be happy to divorce religious traditions from territorial ownership. Let us reflect:

We admire the sunset without thinking 'whose is it?'

> **Mullings**
>
> Dan asks:
> Do Jews and Muslims have an equal claim to the Holy Land?
>
> Peter asks:
> Can Jews and Muslims feel wonder at Jerusalem without thinking 'Mine, all mine'?

Chapter Twelve

Are not Muslims better off in Israel than in Islamic states?

12.1 DAN argues:

According to Israel's Bureau of Statistics, in 2013 the Arab population in Israel was approximately 1,658,000; this represents 20.7% of the population of the country. The majority of these individuals identify themselves as Arab or Palestinian by nationality and Israeli by citizenship. Many have family ties to Palestinians in the West Bank and the Gaza Strip, as well as to Palestinian refugees in Jordan, Syria, and Lebanon. The rights of these citizens are guaranteed by a set of basic Israeli laws. Nonetheless, many Arab citizens believe that the state, as well as society at large, limits them to second-class citizenship and views them as enemies.

The Future Vision of the Palestinian Arabs in Israel is a joint document put together by prominent Arab citizens of Israel in December 2006 that calls for the state of Israel to shed its Jewish identity and become 'a state of all its citizens'. It alleges:

> Defining the Israeli State as a Jewish State and exploiting democracy in the service of its Jewishness excludes us, and creates tension between us and the nature and essence of the State.

This document goes on to explain that, by definition, the 'Jewish State' concept is based on ethnically preferential treatment towards Jews enshrined in immigration and land policy and calls for the establishment of minority rights protections enforced by an independent anti-discrimination commission.

Such claims run counter to the Israeli *Declaration of Independence* which declares that the State of Israel would ensure complete equality of social and political rights to all its inhabitants irrespective of religion, race, or sex, and guarantee freedom of religion, conscience, language, education and culture. However, various official sources acknowledge that the Arab citizens of Israel experience discrimination in many aspects of life.

These are troubling observations about the conditions of a fifth of the population in Israel. Despite the lofty intentions of the early Zionists, the reality is that Arab citizens in Israel face hostility from their Jewish neighbours and in certain respects have limited opportunities. The only viable solution to Jewish-Palestinian conflict is for the Palestinians to have a state of their own where they can enjoy civic equality. Living in other Arab lands – even if freed from such discrimination – is not the solution desired by the Palestinians themselves or their Arab neighbours.

12.2 PETER responds:

Dan, I need to keep the reins on you for, once again, you run off, broadening the debate too quickly. The question is whether Muslims are better off in Israel than in an Islamic state.

The answer must rest on the beliefs of the Muslims in question and the Islamic state in question. The British Muslims that I know – liberal, tolerant – would hate to live in an Islamic state such as Iran or Saudi Arabia. They would find themselves far, far more oppressed than in Israel; they would probably prefer Israel. Of course, their first preference is for a secular-type state – that is probably why they live in North America or Western Europe. Whether the Muslims living under Iranian and Saudi laws would prefer Israeli laws depends in part, I assume, on how conservative their Islamic beliefs are.

Contrast how Israeli laws impinge on its conservative Muslim citizens with how Iranian laws would impinge on Orthodox Jews. My guess is that Muslims in Israel would be better off than Orthodox Jews in Iran.

There is here, I propose, not an antisemitism, but a 'pro-semitism', understood as high expectations that Jewish Israel should perform better regarding non-discriminatory treatments than Islamic countries. I guess that Israel has itself to blame for those expectations because it offers itself as a genuine democracy of citizens with equal rights. There is considerable disappointment when it falls below those standards set.

There is considerable disappointment, but there ought not to be for Israel's existence is immersed in contradiction. It sees itself as a Jewish state yet claims to respect human rights of one and all, without discrimination. Its laws, though, in some areas, discriminate in favour of those committed to Judaism. Its social pressures, customs and habits, tend to give priority to Jews. That is what makes it a Jewish state.

That is indeed what makes it a Jewish state; and while some liberal Muslims may well prefer life in Israel than in any typical Islamic state, it is a myth to insist that an explicit Jewish state can be completely committed to equality of human

> **'What if we win?'**
>
> Israel's economy is in a bad way. Inflation is rising and Jewish immigrants are flooding in from all over the world. What should the country do? The Knesset holds a special session. After hours of futile debate, one member, Yitzhak, stands up and says, 'Quiet everyone, I've got the solution. We'll declare war on the United States.'
>
> Everyone starts shouting. 'You're mad! That's crazy!'
>
> 'Hear me out,' says Yitzhak. 'We declare war. We lose. The United States does what she always does when she defeats a country. She rebuilds everything – our highways, airports, shipping ports, schools, hospitals, factories. She lends us money and sends us food aid. Our problems will be over.'
>
> 'Sure,' says Benny, another minister, 'that's if we lose. But what if we win?'

rights and neutral between how Jews would wish to live and how Muslims and others would wish to live.

12.3 DAN clarifies:

You make a number of references to Israel being a Jewish state. This is crucial to this discussion, so possibly I ought to make several points. From the outset, Jews sought to establish a homeland for world Jewry in the Holy Land. According to Theodor Herzl, this is of fundamental importance. He believed that the problem of antisemitism is insolvable if Jews live as a minority group amongst a majority population. In his view, Jewish persecution and suffering has been an inevitable consequence of nearly two thousand years of exile from their ancient homeland. The Zionist movement was predicated on the assumption that Jews will not be secure unless they live together in a Jewish state.

Some Zionists (like Martin Buber) agitated for the creation of a single state composed of Jews and Arabs (as opposed to a Jewish state). Yet, such an idealistic notion was rejected by the Zionist establishment. In their view, it was imperative that Israel serve as a refuge for Jews. Since the early nineteenth century this has been the central aim of the vast majority of Jews living in Israel and the diaspora. Nonetheless, there are today some Jewish proponents of a one-state solution combining both Jews and Palestinians. But such a political stance has gained little support.

Of course, Israel being a Jewish state inevitably has deleterious consequences for the very large number of Arabs living in the Holy Land. Israeli Arabs (whether Muslim or Christian) suffer from various disabilities and restrictions. This is partly because they are considered a potential threat to the security of the state. Arabs view their predicament as a manifestation of deep-seated prejudice. In defence of Israeli policy, Zionists focus on the dangers presented by Arabs living in their midst.

You may be unaware that the Israeli Law of Return allows all Jews to settle in Israel. Palestinians, and Palestinian Muslims living in Britain or elsewhere, do not have the right to settle in Israel as all Jews can. But, even if Palestinians were permitted to settle in Israel under the Law of Return, they would not be happy with the current state of affairs.

12.4 PETER ponders further:

Well, Dan, we are agreed that Israel is a Jewish state and, in various respects, discriminates against non-Jews. That particularly hits Muslims within and outside Israel. Nonetheless, my guess is that many easy-going liberal Muslims in Britain would prefer life in Israel than in Iran or Saudi Arabia.

Some people stress that Arabs are free from discrimination in states such as Iran and Saudi; and that contrasts with Arabs in Israel. That, though, merits no stress at all. Woe betide Muslim women,

Are not Muslims better off in Israel than in Islamic states? 157

in Iran, who demand equal rights with men – and the freedom to wear what they like. Woe betide individuals who seek same-sex sexual relationships. Compared with Iran and Saudi, Israel is far more tolerant of different versions of Islam and, for that matter, of Christianity and Judaism.

Win and lose

'Whenever we win, we end up losing.'

As I speculated earlier with my suggestion of 'pro-semitism', the spotlight is aimed at Israel because we expect so much better of it compared with today's Muslim states. Of course, that expectation is silly if of non-discrimination. Once a state is grounded in a particular religion or ethnicity, it is inherently discriminatory. The degree of discrimination varies upon the extent to which the religion is allowed to 'bite'. Israel bites less deeply on its inhabitants than does Iran.

Let us not simper too lovingly over liberal democracies such as the United States and Great Britain, where racial discrimination, sexual discrimination, religious discrimination – all manner of discriminations – are, in the main, outlawed. Obviously, in those arenas, such Western countries are radically better than Islamic states and a little better than Israel. We should, though, remember that socially – in the streets, in the work place – there remains plenty of discrimination, sometimes against Jews, sometimes against Muslims, often against the poor and powerless.

There is a puzzle – a muddle – over where to draw lines between justified and unjustified discriminations. That puzzle is much to the fore in Israel. Israel constitutionally seeks to be a liberal democracy, valuing equal rights, yet – let us not tip-toe around – it is, though, a state expressly created for Jews and Judaism. I picture it as a tug-of-war, a conflict within the nation, where sometimes the equality side is pulling more, sometimes the Judaic side.

12.5 DAN muses on:

I think you are right about the problems of living in an Arab society dominated by Sharia law. Far better to live in a liberal democracy which is tolerant of religious and ethnic differences. We are truly fortunate to live in the West, where our freedoms are guaranteed by law. This is certainly not the case in many Middle Eastern countries. And you are right that, despite discriminatory policies against Palestinians, Israel seeks to provide its citizens with a wide range of civic rights. In this respect, it largely resembles democracies such as those in Europe and elsewhere.

So far, we have been discussing life for Arabs in Israel. But what about life in Gaza and the West Bank? In 2006 Hamas won elections in Gaza. The following year a unity government between Hamas and Fatah collapsed. Eventually, Israel and Egypt sealed Gaza on the grounds that Fatah was unable to provide security. Of the 1.5 million inhabitants, 1.1 million are refugees. The unemployment rate in the Gaza Strip is 40.8%. On average, about 4,500 people live on every square kilometre. The UN reports that there is a shortage of 70,000 housing units due to natural population growth, as well as the damage caused by Israel's ground offensive in 2008–2009. Some 12,000 people are displaced because of the destruction of their homes. Power-cuts are an everyday occurrence.

The situation in the West Bank is equally bleak. In June 1967 the West Bank and East Jerusalem were captured by Israel; the West Bank was not annexed by Israel but placed under Israeli military control until 1982. As a result of the Israeli-Egyptian peace treaty, the West Bank was transported into a semi-civil authority operating under the Israeli Ministry of Defence. The area is now surrounded by a West Bank barrier consisting of a network of fences with vehicle barrier trenches surrounded by an exclusion area which is, on average, 60 metres wide, and concrete walls of up to 8 metres high. It is located mainly within the West Bank, partly along the 1949 Armistice line between the West Bank and Israel.

So, life for Palestinians both in the West Bank and in Gaza is bleak because of Israel's policies.

12.6 PETER resorts to virtues in others and heroism:

Yes, life in Gaza and the West Bank is undoubtedly dreadful. Ideally – or at least as steps to the ideal – radical improvements in water, power and other infrastructures would be undertaken, as also improvements in education and employment opportunities; ugly walls would be destroyed. In reality, Israel focuses on itself. In reality, Arab nations and Muslim groups urge Israel's destruction.

Both sides are at fault – especially their leaderships. We must emphasize the asymmetry again: many Muslims and Arabs want to drive the Jews out completely. Israelis and Jews are not seeking to drive out Muslims and Arabs. Yet, yes, something must be done. Here is the 'something' again.

Israel could urge its Western supporters to invest in Gaza and the West Bank. Instead of being ever ready to flex its military muscles against Palestinian protests, Israel could take risks and relax borders. It could act in a spirit of generosity, of fellow-feeling – and in hope of that spirit being respected. Of course, it is easy for Peter Cave, in London's safety, to say that something must be done, especially when my 'something' is the pulling down of walls, engagement in trade and so forth, thus generating big risks to Jewish safety.

Underlying this chapter's question is the fundamental problem of states with religious or ethnic biases. Such states will give priority to those of the 'right' religion or ethnicity. Israel, in fact, offers preferential treatment to the Hasidic Jews, so that the men can study, receiving some welfare benefits, instead of taking paid employment.

There also exists draft deferment from the army for them. All that increasingly does not go down well with the secular Israelis.

Religious or ethnic states, in some ways, will oppress those who reject the religion or lack the ethnicity. If the states have some degree of democracy, those oppressed may one day – perhaps through majority votes, when population ratios change – jettison the religiously grounded laws. We should not, then, smugly believe that our secular democracies are safely stable. Citizens could – through democratic votes – introduce discriminations of Sharia Law. If democratic structures, though, prohibit liberal laws being cast aside, then citizens committed to religious laws are as oppressed, it may be said, as non-believers are in theocracies, in religiously-grounded states such as Iran.

We defenders of liberal democracies may take the heroic path of insisting that certain liberties are essential for human flourishing. Walking that path, I have argued that – to some degree – Muslim citizens within Israel are better off than in Islamic states: liberal Muslims are not remotely so oppressed. In Israel, conservative Muslims, although perhaps not appreciating it, are better off living in a relatively tolerant society than in one that enforces religiously-guided behaviour, even if in accord with their conservative beliefs. Liberties are superior in Israel than in typical

Islamic states, but we may yet have little sympathy for Israel's reality as it impinges on many. We shall see.

> **Mullings**
>
> Dan asks:
> Is life for Palestinians better in Israel or in Arab countries?
>
> Peter asks:
> Can any state which gives priority to a religion be a genuine liberal democracy?

Chapter Thirteen

Does Israel deserve to lose the sympathy vote to the Palestinians?

13.1 DAN argues:

I begin this chapter with a quotation from Uri Avnery's "In Praise of Emotion" in which he argues that peace needs to include an emotional component:

> An Arab villager spoke quietly of his daughter, killed by a soldier on her way to school. A Jewish mother spoke of her soldier son, killed in one of the wars. All in a subdued voice. Without pathos. Some spoke Hebrew, some Arabic.
>
> They spoke of their first reaction after their loss, the feelings of, the thirst for revenge. And then the slow change of heart. The understanding that the parents on the other side, the Enemy, felt exactly like them, that their loss, their mourning, their bereavement was exactly as their own.

For years now, bereaved parents of both sides have been meeting to find solace in each other's company. Among all the peace groups acting in the Israeli-Palestinian conflict, they are, perhaps, the most heart-lifting.

Some of my Jewish friends take sides: they believe the Jews deserve the greater degree of sympathy for their plight. They point to the history of Arab hostility to the creation of a Jewish state, and the determination of the Arab world to drive the Jewish population into the sea. Others, my Palestinian friends, are equally vocal about what they perceive as the evils of the Israeli government. In their view, Zionists are usurpers of their land and murderers of their loved ones. They believe it is the Palestinians, not the Israelis, who deserve sympathy and understanding.

I am loath to take sides. What is needed instead is understanding of both the Israeli and Palestinian arguments and the quest for a peaceful resolution. What is urgently required at this stage of the conflict between Israel and the Palestinians is understanding and forgiveness.

13.2 PETER responds:

Dan, you express feelings for both 'sides' of the Israeli/Palestinian conflict; you emphasize how both parties need to be empathetic. I agree: I said earlier on, pithily:

> It is simple, dear Palestinians and Jews, just manifest generosity and empathy.

My pith, though, was tinged with bleak irony, for it is easy to make such 'motherhood and apple-pie' recommendations: 'just' adopt those attitudes. We are so distant from the sufferings of Palestinians, many of whom are virtually 'caged in' by Israeli actions. We are so distant from Israeli Jews, many of whom are fearful of rocket attacks and well aware that opponents would wish for their complete elimination. True, a few brave souls on both sides, there in the lands, risk calling for empathy and reconciliation.

Typically, Arab leaders do not help matters; they fan flames of hatred against Jews. Many Jewish leaders do not help matters; criticisms of Israeli policies receive shrill accusations of antisemitism.

With your focus on empathy and forgiveness, I infer that your core answer to the chapter's question is that both sides require sympathy votes and we ought not to calculate who merits the greater. If I am right, then that, to some extent, harmonizes with my earlier criticism of people who stress rights, in particular rights of territorial ownership.

'Rights' talk encourages the 'black or white' attitude; it is often associated with Immanuel Kant's thoughts on the demands of duty, of justice. That contrasts with ethical approaches grounded in the virtues and flourishing lives, approaches derived from ancient Greek philosophers, notably Aristotle. The neo-Aristotelian 'virtue' ethics recognizes that flourishing involves having the right feelings towards others, being motivated by compassion, benevolence and generosity – though not too much, points out Aristotle. Ever with his feet firmly on the grounds of realism, Aristotle would not recommend letting your generosity lead to your poverty.

Urging understanding and empathy, Uri Avnery utters fine words. Dan Cohn-Sherbok, Peter Cave and many others utter fine words. With such finery flying around us, questions are blown into view. First, how do we tempt Middle Eastern leaderships to utter the fine words? Secondly, how do we coax those leaderships to have right feelings behind the fine words and act on them? Thirdly – and this is the essential difficulty – how do we even know which actions best manifest those fine words?

13.3 DAN proposes:

You are right, of course, that it is easy for us, living in England, to make recommendations. We are not personally scarred by the history of the Palestinian-Israeli conflict. We are far from the sufferings. Yet, it is imperative that the bloodshed ends, and that Palestinians and Israelis live together in peace. But how is this to be done? As you know, negotiations are fraught with difficulties. Both sides have been intransigent about their demands. But, it seems to me that progress can be made if there are serious and painful compromises.

    A Two-State solution, which I believe is the only possible resolution to the Palestine-Israeli conflict, must grapple with the right of return since this is of fundamental importance. If this is extended to Palestinians, who should have such a right? And where should returning refugees be allowed to settle? Assuming that a Palestinian state were established in the West Bank and Gaza Strip, what should be done about the refugees? Despite subsequent disagreements between Israel and the Palestinians, the 2000 Camp David summit possibly points the way.

    So as not significantly to alter Israeli life, the Palestinian negotiators promised that the right to return would be implemented by a formula agreed by both sides, which would channel a

More sympathy for Jews – or for Palestinians? 169

large number of refugees away from the option of returning to their ancestral home. Nonetheless, each refugee would have the right to return to Israel. It was envisaged that the Palestinians who chose to return to Israel could do so gradually, with Israel absorbing 150,000 refugees a year.

Dog?

A Palestinian gentleman was walking on the West Bank when he was brutally beaten by Israeli thugs. Deciding to take matters into his own hands, he bought a huge German Shepherd trained to kill – and went out to seek revenge. It didn't take him long to see the perfect victim: a little old Jewish man walking a little dog that resembled a dachshund.

The Palestinian let go of his ferocious dog, but to his astonishment he saw the little dog pin his big dog down to the ground and swallow it full, all in thirty seconds.

'What kind of dog is that?' asked the Palestinian, shaking and shocked.

'Dog? Well, before we had his nose fixed he was an alligator!' With that, the old man wandered off, canine alligator in tow yet somewhat bloated with his surprise meal.

The Israel negotiators, concerned that such an influx, as put forward above, would undermine the character of the Jewish state, proposed that a maximum of 100,000 refugees each year should be allowed entry. All other Palestinian refugees should be settled in their current place of residence (either other countries or a Palestinian state), and Israel would help fund their absorption. It seems to me that the positions outlined by both the Palestinians and the Israeli negotiators could serve as a framework for future negotiations.

13.4 PETER ponders further:

You have faith, dear Dan, in the peace framework proposed at Camp David. I lack faith. I doubt if peace would flow even if the leaderships agreed to a Palestinian 'right of return' to Israel of 100,000 each year. As long as Israelis and Palestinians understand their respective national identities as *exclusively* grounded in the Holy Land, the essential conflict persists.

My disposition is to accept that typically we have to muddle through. In the abstract world of mathematics, we have clear definitions distinguishing triangles from squares and evens from odds. In earthly reality, there are grey areas, fudges, not sharp boundaries, between red and orange, reckless and reasonable – and the rights and wrongs of Jewish and Palestinian claims to the Holy Land. Both sides, though, seem to think it is 'black or white'.

Both sides need to be nudged away from the 'black or white'. The start, as already urged, could be for Israel to show some generosity of spirit; after all, Israel has the greater power and is losing the international sympathy vote.

Consider Gaza, which relies heavily on humanitarian aid. The people there, as you note, are mostly young and unemployed. A few have earnings, but mainly through Palestinian/Islamic or Hamas military forces. Suppose – and here I use the thinking of Sara Roy, a major academic authority on Gaza – suppose that Israel took a risk: it sets up some technological industries by Gaza, employs Gazans, makes travel less restricted, promotes the products internationally as 'Made in Gaza' – and aims eventually to place the businesses under Gazan control.

Although there would undoubtedly be security risks for Israel, there would also be potential benefits of Gazans focusing once again on their families' well-being and futures instead of fighting Israel. The rhetoric may persist of how one day Jerusalem must be under Islamic control, but that may gradually slide into paying lip-service to the past, to wistful memories of grandparents.

Were there the Gazan improvements resulting from Israeli help – and similar in the West Bank – then Israel may once again receive some international sympathy. It certainly would deserve to receive such, if the opening of trade and development led to abuse by way of more Palestinian attacks.

13.5 DAN retorts:

I know you believe in muddling through. But, as you yourself note, there are some cases where nudging and fudging won't work. I fear the Israeli-Palestinian conflict is one of them. Both sides apply moral concepts (such as justice) to the political situation and arrive at different conclusions. The stumbling block to a negotiated solution is the clash of these religious and political assumptions and principles. There is a Zionist narrative about the history of modern Israel which is in direct conflict with the Palestinian narrative. There is no space here for what you call 'fudge'.

Let me turn to the policy you outline at the end of your last exchange. You cannot honestly expect the Israeli government to adopt the policy you outline in Gaza as the first steps toward reconciliation. This is completely unrealistic. It will never happen. Instead, both Israelis and Palestinians must be willing to set aside their religious and political principles and work toward a resolution of the conflict. You might think that this is exactly what you propose – a muddling through approach. But it is not. Rather, both sides would be required to suspend their interpretative narratives in the quest for peace.

Identity Parade

Dog?

Some time ago, I wrote a book, *The Palestinian State: A Jewish Justification*, in which I argued that we Jews, as an empowered people, must now strive to help Palestinians establish a state of their own. In his preface to my book, the Palestinian scholar Dawoud El-Alami emphasizes that both sides must seek to empathize with each other in the quest for peace. If they argue their case on the basis of history and morality, they will get nowhere. This is not a case of nudge and fudge, or muddling through. Instead, El-Alami's recommendation is that both sides seek to transcend their principles and instead seek to gain compassion for the other. Do you agree? Or do you think a different approach is required?

13.6 PETER sighs:

I had a feeling that you would be unhappy with my 'nudge', 'fudge' and 'muddling through', yet you argue that both sides need 'to suspend their interpretative narratives in the quest for peace'. That sounds like fudging matters – for 'the suspension' – but, if it helps, I mind not at all in assenting to your highfalutin terminology. After all, you are a rabbi, and I, but a humble philosopher.

Mind you, it is odd and depressing that El-Alami and you apparently believe that basing solutions on Islamic and Judaic morality will get us nowhere; that, instead, the focus must be on compassion and empathy. Morality, I would argue, very much involves acting with compassion, empathy and other virtues. I viewed both Islam and Judaism as recognizing such virtues and understanding them as essential to morality.

Blind as I must be, I cannot see (!) how my suggestion of Israel manifesting a generosity of spirit in helping Palestinians to prosper is any more unrealistic than your saying that both Israelis and Palestinians must be willing to set aside religious and political principles – save that my suggestion is also for some practical help to be done right now. Instead of unemployed young Palestinians lacking all hope, except the 'hope' fed by Hamas and similar, my picture would have them employed, with aspirations for family life, for prosperity offered by education, culture, travel – and even international football.

Allow me to end this chapter again with 'the bigger picture'. Whatever Holy Land arrangements are made tomorrow, next year, or in the next decade, is there not an intrinsic instability if Israel insists on discriminating in favour of Jews, and Palestine in favour of Muslims? What happens if or when the Muslim Palestinians outnumber the Jews in Israel? Even if Israeli policies ensure that Israel itself always maintains a significant majority of Jews within its borders, what happens when outside of those borders, in Gaza and in the West Bank, there are ever-increasing millions of dispossessed Palestinians? In such a case, it is surely a desperate hope that, in your terms, Dan, the Palestinians and/or Muslims – and the Jewish Israelis – would be willing to suspend their 'interpretative narratives' of the disputed lands.

While Israel does not currently receive much by way of the sympathy vote – and ought not to – give it a few more decades, with my speculative population changes above, and Israel may well be in need of huge sympathy. My hope, also probably forlorn, is that the past, be it Islamic, be it Judaic, does not continue to hold so much sway over future generations. And my immediate thought, also swaddled in forlornness, is: forget about 'interpretative narratives' for peace; instead, Israel, do something – help the surrounding Palestinians to prosper.

Mullings

Dan asks:
  Should political problems be solved by suspension of interpretative narratives?

Peter asks:
  For peace in the Holy Land, must not Jews, Muslims and Palestinians unburden themselves with the past?

Chapter Fourteen
Boycotts: should we stop buying Israel's avocados, dates and pomegranates?

14.1 DAN argues:

Boycotts of Israel are a systematic practice of avoiding economic, political and cultural ties with the State of Israel. Boycott campaigns are used by those who oppose Israel's very existence, or its policies regarding the Palestinians. They have been enacted or proposed around the world and involve economic measures such as divestment or boycotts of Israeli products or businesses. In addition, there have been boycotts of Israeli universities. Some advocates of boycotts use the 1980's movement against South African apartheid as a model.

Defenders of Israel have denounced the boycott campaign. The Anti-Defamation League, for example, has claimed that singling out Israel is outrageous and biased, and the heads of various major US Jewish organizations have referred to the boycott campaign as lop-sided and unbalanced. Critics of boycotts have also argued that those in support of these campaigns are using a false analogy with the previous apartheid policy of South Africa.

What are we to make of this situation? There is clearly a fundamental distinction between South African apartheid and the Israeli treatment of Palestinians. Although the free movement of Palestinians in the West Bank and Gaza is regulated by Israel, the territories are governed by the Palestinian Authority and Hamas. In South Africa, racial segregation policies were enshrined in law, whereas there is no parallel with Israeli law. Nonetheless, as we have repeatedly noted, Israel privileges Jewish citizens and in effect discriminates against Arab citizens of the state.

But are boycotts the way forward? In my view, a just and peaceful solution to the Israeli-Palestinian problem can only be achieved through negotiation and compromise. Boycotts only inflame conflict. They do not provide a framework for mutual understanding, reconciliation and the creation of a Palestinian state. In the past, Israeli and Palestinian negotiators failed to reach agreement over a wide range of issues because they were unwilling to make substantial compromises. But if progress is to be made, this must be done. You have suggested muddling through on the way to agreement. Instead, I have stressed the importance of empathy.

14.2 PETER responds:

Well, Dan, once again, you highlight the need for empathy – as have I, though I also urge the need for Israel to act now, with generosity of spirit. Israel's lack of generous action probably makes the boycott calls more persuasive. What, though, is the boycott's aim? Is it likely to achieve the aim?

To the first question, no doubt boycotters have a variety of aims, dependent upon the intensity and arena of boycott. A credible aim is to highlight to many Israelis – as the protesting Israelis do – that much of the international community is distressed by the Israeli mistreatment of Palestinians and appalled at Israel's flouting of various humanitarian conventions and United Nations' resolutions. Israel's actions damage Israel's reputation and that of Jews more widely.

To the second question, I doubt if the small attempted boycotts, be they of fruit or academic interchange, make much difference for, as said, there is already internal protest against Israel's Palestinian policies. Things would be different, if boycotts intensified. If the United States and related countries ceased all support for Israel – boycotting all financial, trading and cultural links – that would certainly be a game-changer (I believe that is a favoured term these days). Such a boycott would make a huge difference, but, given the current rhetoric and claims on the Palestinian side and by the Arabs more generally, that could well lead to a Middle East holocaust.

Once again – if I dare use the words – the best that can be done is through the muddle of some nudging here, some fudging there. Possibly some slightly more serious and intensive boycotts in various arenas might impress on the Israeli Jews that they need to remake some gestures of reconciliation towards the Palestinians. I agree that even gestures come with risks. I agree not least because Palestinian leaderships seem to have taken advantage of previous Israeli relaxations; they have taken advantage by increasing violent attacks on Israel.

Whether limited boycotts of Israel would open Israeli eyes more widely, I do not know. I suppose they could aggravate the Israeli belief that an international antisemitism exists.

14.3 DAN proposes:

Let me refer to a speech by Prime Minister Benjamin Netanyahu, delivered to the UN following President Mahmoud Abbas's address there on 23 September 2011. Netanyahu extended the hand of peace to the Palestinian people yet stressed that peace must be anchored in security. The truth, he stated, is that a solution to the Middle East crisis cannot be achieved through UN resolutions, but only through direct negotiations between the parties. Israel, he insisted, wants peace with a Palestinian state, but the Palestinians want a state without peace.

For Jews the security of Israel is paramount. After nearly 2000 years of exile, we have returned to the land of our ancestors. Such a hope sustained the Jewish people through centuries of suffering and persecution. Nonetheless, in our determination to protect our ancestral home, we must not abandon the spiritual tradition that calls us to liberate those who are currently in bondage. The Jewish prophetic tradition highlights concern for human dignity. The Exodus that we celebrate at Passover reminds us of the eternal obligation to help the oppressed and enslaved. Jewish ethics is a morality of praxis, of concrete action in the present. We must not stand aloof from human degradation. As an empowered people, it is our duty to empower those who remain in exile, as we were for nearly twenty centuries.

> ### The Sign
>
> A rabbi is walking down the street in New York when he is shocked by a sign in front of a building. The sign reads:
>
> **We prefer business with 1000 Hamas terrorists than with any Israeli.**
>
> Enraged, the rabbi walks up to the building, to yell in disgust at the owners, but he suddenly stops; he notices a smaller sign:
>
> **THE CHEVRA KADISHA (Hebrew Burial Society)**

It is true that within the Jewish community there are those who are unbending. Some religious Jews, for example, cite the scriptural account of God's promise to Abraham that his descendants would inherit the land as a basis for their conviction that the Holy Land belongs exclusively to the Jews. Yet, other central themes in Scripture emphasize the need for compassion. It is these key elements, I believe, that can serve as a framework for peace. But for this to be accomplished, there must be intense serious negotiations that call for painful compromise on the part of both Israel and the Palestinians. To use a biblical image, it is time to turn swords into ploughshares, before it is too late.

14.4 PETER sighs:

Once again, you speak of the need for compassion, understanding and reconciliation. I do too, but it all sounds 'apple-pie-ish' – and not directly related to boycotts.

My eagerness to promote generosity of spirit contrasts, as I recognize, with the determination by many Jews, be they Judaic or atheistic, be they living within Israel or without, that they must not yield what they now have acquired of the Holy Land, not least because of their need for security – despite the United Resolutions calling for certain withdrawals. I seek to reconcile generosity of spirit with that determination regarding territorial ownership by...?

Yes, I fill in those dots with: 'muddling through'. True, those convinced that any relaxation of borders will lead to Israel's annihilation are unlikely to welcome my muddling. My hunch, though, is that 'muddling' *et al* may have a slightly more 'user-friendly' ring to most than 'compromise' which sounds formal and definite.

184 *Jews: Nearly Everything You Wanted to Know*

A few chapters ago, I was somewhat mocked for suggesting that maybe Jews could forget a little of their past, of harsh readings of the Torah and so forth – but that suggestion is not so different from your line on compromise, Dan. My line is to urge that all those debates about the correct renderings of Judaism, its scriptures and traditions, be put on the backburner. Instead, let us attend to the current circumstances where most Palestinians feel a hopelessness in their lives and where many Israeli Jews feel under constant threat of elimination.

The Chevra Kadisha

'*Torah,* Shulhan Arukh, *shop signs – oy vey, all must be read closely.*'

My proposal, to repeat, is that Israel takes some steps, not without risk, to invest in Gaza and the West Bank, thus providing employment and prospects and hopes. I suggest that Israel sets about this with some humility, with regrets for the current awful state of affairs, with international declarations that it is doing so, not least in the hope that the publicity of such generosity may (*may*) discourage Hamas *et al* from taking advantage – and may secure international sympathy.

The above proposal is allied to the belief that squabbles between Israel and Gaza about how to organize the supply of avocados, dates and pomegranates to the outside world are far better than, and may distract from, threatening disputes about who owns Jerusalem. Those disputes might just possibly be better handled once Palestinians and Israelis find themselves engaged in mutually beneficial trade and – returning us to this chapter's topic – such a beneficial trade would then mean that calls for boycotts of Israel become inappropriate and silly.

14.5 DAN acknowledges:

You are right that our discussion has veered away from the topic of boycotts of Israel and right to return us to the subject. You make a plea for religion to be set on one side in the Israel-Palestinian dispute. I think you are partially right. A number of strictly Orthodox Jews and others have made the case on scriptural grounds that the Holy Land belongs exclusively to the Jews. In this light, they argue that the government should make no compromises with Palestinians. It is they, rather than the Jews, who are usurpers.

Such an intransigent stance has made it impossible for negotiators to engage in fruitful discussion. This does not mean, however, that religious conviction should play no role in attempting to reach a just and peaceful solution to the Middle-East conflict. I have argued in this chapter that there are considerable resources for empathy and compassion within the Jewish tradition. Arguably, it is these elements of our heritage which can have a profound influence on Jewish consciousness.

Boycotts of Israel, on the other hand, lead only to friction, hostility and violence. As you may be aware, 45 US senators supported a bill that would make boycotting Israel a crime. The so-called 'Israel Anti-Boycott Act' would impose fines of up to $250,000 on any US citizen engaged in interstate or foreign commerce who supports a boycott of Israeli goods and services. Such a bill was proposed in the light of America's defence of Israel despite the country's expansion into areas assigned to the Palestinians by international law.

Such a bill would run counter to the position of the United Nations which claims Israel's settlements in occupied Palestinian territory have no legal validity and constitute a flagrant violation of international law. Nonetheless, in their legislation the members of Congress who support this bill point out that the UN is considering a resolution to withhold assistance from and prevent trade with settlements in East Jerusalem, the West Bank and the Golan Heights. The Israeli Anti-Boycott Act is designed to punish any American who supports such measures.

14.6 PETER concludes:

Unsurprisingly, we have reached little agreement or even disagreement over boycotts – not least, dare I say, because you have said little about them, Dan, until just now. You reject boycotts because they 'lead to conflict and misunderstanding'. I reply: sometimes there can be beneficial outcomes of conflict and even misunderstandings.

There were boycotts – from sport to banking – of apartheid South Africa. By keeping South Africa's racism high on the international agenda, they perhaps contributed to the overthrow of apartheid. We could also point to small local boycotts of firms mistreating their employees; they sometimes secure better employment conditions.

Talk of boycotting Israel, and actual small boycotting gestures, at least help to keep Israel's Palestinian policies in the news. My earlier suggestions, if followed, of Israel investing in Gaza, trading Gazan goods and so forth, would undermine calls for trading boycotts – and would return sympathy for Israel, were Hamas to intensify attacks on Israel.

Let me close this discussion, though, by noting how boycotts link to the collective responsibility that we discussed earlier.

Boycotts are typically aimed at a group – in this case, the Israeli nation because of Israel's Palestinian policies. Some Israelis actively oppose those policies; consequently, by harming the group, a boycott harms some innocent members of that group. There are calls for boycotts of Israeli universities, yet many who would be adversely affected are lecturers and students who protest against the relevant Israeli policies.

As is not unusual, we often close our eyes to unjust treatments of innocents; they are unfortunate side-effects of actions aimed at some beneficial outcomes. Ought we to close eyes? In fact, we often mutter about difficult decisions and how it is a matter of degree. That innocent people are harmed is something we try to forget or describe as 'collateral damage'. On a much larger scale than boycotts, witness the deliberate attacks by both Israel and Palestine – by the United States and Russia in the Middle East – that kill or maim totally innocent civilians.

Should we stop buying Israel's avocados, dates and pomegranates? Well, if it helps to encourage Israel to improve the lives of Palestinians, then 'Yes'. Let us not ignore the fact, though, that, in the short term, we may be harming innocent farmers and suppliers of the avocados, dates and pomegranates – but we had better try to close our eyes to that.

Mullings

Dan asks:
 Do boycotts help resolve a political conflict or make matters worse?

Peter asks:
 Is it ever right wittingly to harm the innocent for the possibility of a long-term greater good?

Part Three
Israel, integrity and reasons to wail

Chapter Fifteen
Can Israel be a Jewish state – and if so, for how long?

15.1 DAN argues:

For the Palestinians, the concept of Israel as a Jewish state is anathema. Such a stance is based on the determination to ensure that Palestinians would, like Jews, have the same right of return. In support of his opposition to recognizing Israel as a Jewish state, the President of the Palestinian Authority, Mahmoud Abbas, stated in January 2014:

> The Palestinians won't recognize the Jewishness of the State of Israel and won't accept it. The Israelis say that if we don't recognize the Jewishness of Israel there will be no solution. And we say that we won't recognize or accept the Jewishness of Israel and we have many reasons for this rejection.

The Israeli government, however, is determined that Israel should be a Jewish state, fearing that the Palestinian Authority seeks to establish a Palestinian state next to Israel while at the same time flooding Israel with millions of refugees. From its nineteenth-century beginnings, the Zionist movement was determined to create a Jewish state in the ancient homeland. After centuries of persecution, the Zionists were convinced that Jewish survival could only be assured if the Jewish people had a country of their own. That conviction remains a fundamental principle of Zionism.

Here, then, is a major impasse which has beleaguered all negotiations in the past and is currently central in the debate about Israel's future. Is there a solution? There can be a way forward only if both sides are willing to make major concessions. Jews will never give up the determination that Israel is a Jewish state. Yet, at the same time, it is vital that the Israeli government grant the right of return to Palestinians in some fashion. Previously, Palestinian negotiators perceived the difficulties of massive immigration to Israel. What is needed now is for a realistic immigration figure to be accepted by both sides.

15.2 PETER reflects:

Dan, you have read this question as practical: you call for both sides to make concessions, as you have done previously, while pointing out that it is essential to Jews that Israel be Jewish and essential to Palestinians that it be Palestinian. With such entrenched positions, I doubt whether compromises permitting some Palestinian return to Israel would be reached. Even if they were, the Palestinian side would hail them as first steps towards a Palestinian Israel – and that is what the Jews would fear.

Let me provide the best possible scenario of how Israel, as a Jewish state, could survive and not be under threat:

> Suppose Israel to be totally populated by Jews, committed to Judaism. Suppose its borders are under no threat; its neighbours maintain friendly attitudes. Countries trade with Israel – people visit as tourists – but there are no demands by outsiders to live in Israel with citizen rights.

Would that guarantee Jewish Israel's survival? The answer is 'No' – or, more accurately, 'Yes', but only if 'Jew' only means 'anyone descended from Jews'.

I assume that for Israel to be Jewish, it retains Jewish characteristics – perhaps features of Judaism in its laws and customs, respect for synagogues and the Western Wall and so forth. There is, though, no assurance that those features would persist. Today's Jews cannot bind attitudes and beliefs of future Jewish generations. Those generations may dismantle everything Jewish, perhaps turning the Western Wall area into a Disneyland theme park or a Donald Trump golf pitch – sorry, golf course. They may dismiss religion completely; they may convert to Islam.

True, current Israeli Jews could try to indoctrinate the young and newly-born and hence future generations; they could prohibit outside sources of information. The problems with that response are twofold. First, it goes against Judaic commitments to open discussion, thus undermining something importantly Jewish. Secondly, there is no certainty that such repression would be successful; it could well generate protest, a backlash, even catastrophe.

Under my supposition of the very best scenario for a persisting Jewish Israel, there is no certainty that it will last for long. And, of course, the current scenario in which Jewish Israel finds itself is far, far removed from the very best just outlined.

15.3 DAN corrects:

I think there is a fundamental misunderstanding about what is meant by a Jewish state. In the past, there were Zionists who were determined that Israel embody the highest ideals of Judaism. In the same spirit, strictly Orthodox Jews today seek to ensure that religious law is rigorously observed in the Holy Land. Yet, the majority of Jews in Israel and the diaspora have a different vision of what it means for Israel to be Jewish. Far from encouraging Israel to be a theocracy, they are determined that the country is regulated by secular law.

From the late nineteenth century onwards, secular Zionists conceived of Israel as essentially a refuge from persecution. It is to be a bulwark against prejudice and discrimination. In order to ensure that Jews will be secure no matter where they live, the Law of Return provides a means whereby Jews can escape from oppression and suffering. This is what it means for Israel to be a Jewish state. For the Zionist vision to be a reality, it must be so.

That is not to say that Jews living in Israel have turned their backs on the tradition. On the contrary, Hebrew has been adopted as the official language. The Bible and rabbinic sources form part of the school curriculum. Major Jewish festivals are widely observed. But there are significant

> **Emergency meeting of the UN: the latest conflict in the Middle East**
>
> The Israeli Delegate has the floor:
>
> 'Ladies and gentlemen before I commence my speech, I need to relay an old story to all of you.
>
> 'When Moses was leading the Jews out of Egypt, he travelled through deserts, and prairies, and even more deserts... The people became thirsty and needed water. So, Moses struck the side of a mountain with his cane and a pond appeared with clean, cool water. The people rejoiced and drank to their hearts' content.
>
> 'Moses wished to cleanse his body, so he went to the other side of the pond, removed all his clothes, and stepped into the cool waters of the pond. Only when Moses came out of the water, did he discover that all his clothes had gone... And we have excellent reasons for believing that the Palestinians stole his clothes.'
>
> The Palestinian Delegate, hearing this accusation, jumps out of his seat and screams, 'This is a travesty. It is widely known that there were no Palestinians there at the time!'
>
> 'With that in mind', said the Israeli Delegate, 'let me begin my speech...'

numbers of non-Jewish citizens in Israel who are free to observe their own religious rites.

Palestinians, however, repudiate such a conception. Intent on returning to their homes, they view Zionists, with their Law of Return, as usurpers of their country. Yet, they will inevitably fail in seeking to turn Israel into a pluralist society to which Palestinians have the right to emigrate. For two thousand years, Jews have lived as a minority people in foreign lands. After two millennia of wandering from country to country, Jews have returned to their ancient homeland. Nothing will persuade them that Israel must now become a country like every other.

15.4 PETER learns – or does he?

I write corrected, well, confused. You speak of Israel as a secular state, yet also as Jewish. On the latter, yes indeed, for it clearly discriminates in favour of Jews; so, I wonder about its secular – and democratic – credentials.

Suppose Israel is in the best possible circumstances as I outlined earlier, save now it insists that it is both secular and Jewish. So? It remains true that, save by indoctrination, current Israelis cannot bind future Jewish generations. Those future Israeli Jewish generations may repudiate the Law of Return for a variety of reasons, be they economic, social or, for that matter, religious;

200 *Jews: Nearly Everything You Wanted to Know*

A Travesty

'Oops, I didn't mean that...'

they may see it as outmoded racism. Those future generations may even turn against and prohibit Jewish festivals, religious teaching in schools and Orthodox displays in public. Beliefs, attitudes, values – 'things' – change.

Perhaps my next assumption is mistaken, but I assume that when today's Jews value Israel persisting, they are not merely valuing the existence of a certain set of people descended from Jews of Abraham's days. Surely the value of Israel is that it maintains, for example, respect for Jewish traditions, the significance of the Western Wall and remembrance of the horrors of antisemitism.

We are returning to Chapter One's mysteries. If Israel's *sole* importance is to ensure a population of Jewish descent continues, whatever its beliefs and attitudes, then why would it be so important? If, as I suspect, there is a range of characteristics that Jews must maintain to survive 'as Jews', then who knows what is the best way of achieving that? Jews may, for example, have a better chance of retaining their traditions in the liberal West, rather than in a Middle East surrounded by perhaps ever-increasing antisemitic populations.

Let me raise the basic question again. Suppose Israel survives as Jewish, but those future 'Jewish' populations lack all interest in Jewish traditions, beliefs and practices. They turn synagogues into gambling halls. Would you be so keen on the importance of that future Israel and those future generations existing?

15.5 DAN responds:

You raise a key question that is not always directly faced by contemporary Jewry. Why should Israel survive? And for that matter, why should Jews survive? Let me assure you that throughout the Jewish world, there is universal commitment to Jewish survival and the existence of a Jewish state in the Holy Land. These are critical and fundamental assumptions. But why?

The Orthodox answer to these questions is that it is God's will that the Jewish people endure, and that they observe his sacred laws. Such a religious commitment is at the forefront of the traditional Jewish way of life. Orthodoxy maintains that at Mount Sinai, God revealed both the Written and Oral Torah to Moses, and that these divine commandments are binding on all Jews throughout time. They are sacrosanct and must be observed.

Most Jews, however, are much vaguer about the rationale for the survival of the Jewish people and for Israel's continued existence. In general, they view the Jewish state as an ultimate insurance policy. In the light of Jewish history, they share the assumptions of the early Zionists (like Theodor Herzl) that Jews will never be entirely secure in the diaspora. In their view, the Law of Return is crucial because it ensures that every Jew has the opportunity to settle in the Holy Land. What is at stake is not the Jewish religious way of life, but the very existence of Jewry.

You are right that, in the future, Israelis (as well as Jews in the diaspora) may well not share some of the assumptions of past and current generations. No doubt they will have different political and religious views. Yet, I think it is inevitable that they will continue to believe that the existence of Israel is of vital importance. They, too, will not forget the past history of Jewish suffering, and the insecurity of Jews living as a minority people in foreign lands. Whatever their religious or political beliefs, they will remain totally committed to the continued existence of the Jewish state.

15.6 PETER concludes:

You, even though a rabbi, Dan, show commitment to Israel and Jews, even if belief in Judaism is lost. So, I put God to one side. What remains?

Well, you are so amazingly assured that future individuals who happen to have been born of a Jewish mother or a Jewish father are bound, *bound*, to identify themselves as Jewish – that is, as Jewish in the sense of it hugely mattering and not just being a matter of genetic history. Further, they are bound to be totally committed to the existence of a Jewish Israel. Why are you so certain?

You may respond that antisemites keep the Jews united as a people: Jews owe their identity to the enemy without. That has a 'chicken and egg' feel: perhaps Israel's existence encourages the idea to non-Jews that Jews consider themselves as separate and special; that encourages antisemitism; and that justifies preserving Israel's existence which encourages the idea – and so we circle round. It would be odd, though, to believe that Jewish identity has a value that must persist solely because others object to it.

Let us be realistic. We have a small Jewish state, Israel, surrounded by increasing numbers of non-Jews, currently extremely hostile to Jews and Israel. We also have increasing numbers of non-Jews within Israel. Those elements suggest that in centuries to come, Israel as a Jewish state is potentially under attack from without – and from within. They surely are not grounds for believing that Jewish Israel is bound to exist.

I value diversity; I should like to think that the distinctive Jewishness of Israel would continue to exist. No doubt, though, many Romans liked to think that the Roman Empire would persist. No doubt, many Catholics were assured that certain Catholic countries would retain their Catholicism for centuries. Maybe native Indian tribes in North America felt themselves safe.

My point has simply been that things change. Even if Israel, the territory, persists as the grounding of a country, there is no guarantee that it will persist as distinctively Jewish – and we may see this all the more so, when we turn to the topic of liberal democracies.

> **Mullings**
>
> Dan asks:
> Could Israel continue as a Jewish state if its Jewish citizens abandoned the Jewish heritage?
>
> Peter asks:
> Does Israel as a Jewish state merit support as a safe haven for Jews – or condemnation as no better than a racist state?

Chapter Sixteen
Can a Jewish state be a liberal democracy, avoiding apartheid?

16.1 DAN gets us started:

If being an apartheid state means committing inhumane acts, systematic oppression and domination by one racial group over another, then Israel is guilty according to a recent United Nations report. The findings have not been fully backed by the UN leadership and do not set new policies toward Israel. But they nonetheless reflect another attempt to use a UN forum to denounce Israel.

Titled "Israeli Practices Toward the Palestinian People and the Question of Apartheid," the report concluded that Israel had established an apartheid regime aimed at dominating the Palestinians. Recommendations include reviving the UN Centre Against Apartheid which closed in 1994 after South Africa ended its apartheid practices. The

Is Jewish Israel miles away from apartheid? 207

report also urges support for a boycott, divestment and a sanctions campaign against Israel.

Dividing the Palestinian people into four distinct groups, the authors write that although they are treated differently by Israel, they all face racial oppression. The first group identified is the roughly 1.7 million Palestinians who are full citizens of Israel, but who, the report argues, live under 'marital law' and are subject to oppression because they are not Jewish.

The second group highlighted is the estimated 300,000 Palestinians who live in East Jerusalem. The report maintains that these Palestinians experience discrimination in access to education, health care, employment and building rights. The third group includes the 4.6 million Palestinians who live in the West Bank and Gaza. In the West Bank, Jewish residents known as settlers are governed by Israeli civil law, while Palestinians live under military rule. The last group are the millions of Palestinian refugees who live outside Israeli territory and who are prohibited from returning to their homes in Israel or the occupied Palestinian territory.

16.2 PETER reflects:

Apartheid, without nuances, is, as you say, discrimination on grounds of race. Even that generates puzzles, for most argue that there is no clear concept of 'race', yet paradoxically manage to identify some people as racist. Let us simply accept that, typically, we can recognize a distinction between a vast swathe of people who identify as Arabs and a smaller swathe of people who identify themselves as Jews; they recognize themselves as belonging to different groups.

To be so great

During a service in a wealthy synagogue, the rabbi got carried away. Falling on hands and knees, forehead to floor, he said, 'Oh God, before thee I am nothing.'

The Cantor, not to be outdone, also got down, forehead to floor and said, 'Oh God, before thee I am nothing.'

Seeing this, Levy, a tailor in the fourth row, left his seat, fell to his knees, forehead to floor, and he too said, 'Oh God, before thee I am nothing.'

With this, the Cantor elbowed the rabbi and sniffed, 'Look who thinks he's nothing!'

You first mention those Israeli Palestinians with full citizen rights. They suffer discriminations because of Israel's marriage laws. That, though, is a far cry from South Africa's apartheid, the United States' one-time segregation policies and, until more recently, Switzerland's restrictions on women having the vote. Must all countries have the same laws regarding equal treatment? Perhaps they should, but that risks losing interesting and valuable diversities.

You mention three other Palestinian groups arising because of areas that Israel took over, one way or another, in response to the Arab-initiated 1967 war to destroy Israel. That raises many questions concerning post-war settlements, but a relevant question here concerns how liberal democracies handle borders. Few (if any?) countries, let us note, have open borders. With borders imposed, the question becomes, what does (or does not) justify discriminating such that some groups are allowed in, others are not?

Israel has excellent reasons, though not conclusive ones, to set severe limits and restrictions on the entry of non-Jews into its lands. Were it to open its borders to all Palestinians, that would be the end of Jewish Israel. With considerably lower existential danger, Britain and continental Europe keep their borders largely closed to non-Europeans; they turn away economic migrants from Northern Africa. There is a significant difference, many argue. Palestinians have a 'right' to Israeli land; those who flee Syria and Northern Africa have no 'right' to European lands. 'Rights' talk returns us to the unhappy territorial arguments already engaged.

This chapter focuses on the particular problems for Israel when presenting itself as a liberal democracy. Saudi Arabia, Iran, China – and many other countries – do not seriously offer themselves up as democracies; they get away with far worse discriminations than those committed by Israel. Israel, though, sees itself very much as a Western-style liberal democracy – yet also a Jewish state. That generates the highlighted conflict.

To maintain its Jewishness, must not Israel either limit its liberality and democracy or limit the size of its non-Jewish population?

16.3 DAN expands:

You are right: Israel is a serious problem if it is to be a Jewish state in the Middle East. Palestinians believe the Zionists have stolen their land, and they want to return to what they perceive as their ancestral home. Israel, on the other hand, fears a massive influx of Arabs which would displace the

Jewish population. In addition, Jews are aware of Arab hatred. The laws that have been enacted which deprive Palestinians of various rights were formulated to protect Israel from attack. As you say, the State of Israel is surrounded by fierce enemies who are determined to drive the Jewish population into the sea.

Israel is in many respects a liberal democracy governed by law. It aims to protect the rights of all its citizens. But because of political instability, it believes it must protect itself from a hostile presence in its midst. Inevitably, then, Israel is different from other democracies which do not face the same type of political and social problems. Only when Arabs, living within and without Israel, affirm the right of the Jewish state to exist can the obstacles to its being a full democracy be removed. But will this ever be possible? I would like to believe that a Two-State solution will resolve the problem.

One of the key dilemmas in any negotiations is the battle over Jerusalem. During the Arab-Israeli War, West Jerusalem was among the areas annexed by Israel while East Jerusalem, including the Old City, was captured and annexed by Jordan. Subsequently, it was captured by Israel. The international community, however, has regarded the latter annexation as illegal and treats East Jerusalem as Palestinian territory occupied by a foreign power. This ongoing dispute serves as a microcosm of the entire Palestinian-Israeli conflict.

16.4 PETER expands:

You highlight an important factor that distinguishes Israel from other liberal democracies, a factor that may justify those Israeli policies that tarnish its liberal democratic credentials. The factor is 'the enemy within', the enemy being Palestinians who seek Jewish Israel's destruction. In view of the 'enemy within', we should be impressed – at least momentarily – with Israel allowing the 1.7 million Palestinians within its original borders having the vote.

There is a basic inconsistency within most liberal democracies, as shown in, for example, the International Humanist and Ethical Union's 2017 *Freedom of Thought Report* that focuses on treatments of the non-religious. Britain's liberal democracy is tarnished by its 'systemic discrimination' through its state religion and funding of certain religious schools. Israel, on similar measures, displays 'severe discrimination' as does Palestine. Much, much worse are Jordan and other Arab states; they engage in 'grave violations' of human rights.

Knowing one's Judaic place

'Who does he think he is, to think himself nothing?'

The ideal – 'the myth', dare I say? – of a liberal democracy is of a state that upholds the same human rights for all within its territory. Once that state identifies itself, to some extent, as being of one religion or one ethnic group, then it is bound to discriminate. That discrimination may be so mild that basic human rights are not offended; that discrimination may be so strong that the state receives the dubious accolade of 'racist', 'discriminatory' or 'apartheid'.

If we start off with a religious or ethnic state in which all its members are committed to that religion or of that ethnicity, then should we worry? If immigration is permitted, the would-be immigrants, if of a different religion or ethnicity, should know what they will encounter, and accept it on the 'when in Rome' basis. Of course, Israel, America and Britain are not in that position; they lack homogeneity within. In fact, most countries have minority groups that have suffered or do suffer from varying degrees and types of adverse discrimination. While Israel remains a Jewish state, the non-Jewish, as said, are bound to be adversely affected. The question is: to what extent?

Curiously, you argue, Dan, that once there is no Arab threat, then all could be well for Israel as a true liberal democracy. However benign the Palestinians and Muslims within and without Israel become, I ask again how can Israel not have its 'liberal democracy' credentials tarnished, if it is truly a *Jewish* state and ensures that it remains such?

16.5 DAN responds:

You are right: Israel does in some ways fall short of being a liberal democracy. I have been focusing on the ways in which Israel might improve. But I want to return to the vexed question of whether Israel is an apartheid state. According to a 2009 study of Israel's practices in the Occupied Territories, the practices fall almost entirely within the definition of apartheid as established in Article 2 of the International Convention on the Suppression and Punishment of the Crime of Apartheid.

The Israeli practices, the study showed, included violations of internal standards for due process, discriminatory privileges based on ethnicity, enforced ethnic segregation, comprehensive restrictions of individual freedoms, a dual legal system, and a system of laws designed selectively to punish Palestinian resistance to the Israeli system.

Opponents of that comparison argue that such conclusions are prejudicial. In their view, it is antisemitic to label Israel an apartheid state because it implicitly calls for a dismantling of that state.

In recent years, a number of governments have taken steps to challenge the comparison between South Africa and Israel. In March 2001, the Mayor of Toronto, Rob Ford, said that he would not allow city funding for the 2011 Toronto Pride Parade if organizers allowed the group 'Queers Against Israel Apartheid' to march. Former US Ambassador to the United Nations, Daniel Patrick Moynihan, voiced the strong disagreement of the

United States with the General Assembly's resolution declaring that 'Zionism is a form of racism and racial discrimination.'

It is clear that there is considerable disagreement about how Israel's treatment of the Palestinians should be viewed. Yet, despite such differing interpretations, there is no question that full liberal democracy respecting the rights of all citizens is a goal which has not been reached. Only when peace is established between Jews and Arabs will Israel be able to extend full citizenship rights to its Arab population.

16.6 PETER concludes:

Well, Dan, you close with, 'Only when peace is established between Jews and Arabs will Israel be able to extend full citizenship rights to all.'

I shall resist – and hence once again not resist – noting that obviously Israel 'can' at any stage extend full citizen rights to all. I assume that you mean that only when peace exists would it be prudent for Israel to serve up such an extension. You may also mean that not doing so at present is morally justified because it is a form of Israeli self-defence. Self-defence, though, is only morally justified if what one defends is a good – and that returns us to the rights and wrongs of Israel's territorial ownership and whether the existence of a Jewish Israel is a good.

The survival of a Jewish state may, indeed, be a good; but if it is, then we are accepting that being a full liberal democracy, with no discriminations whatsoever based on religion and ethnicity, is not overwhelmingly important. As argued earlier, any religious- or ethnicity-based state, to some degree, lacks a fully blown liberal democracy. We ought not to be surprised.

We may be surprised, though, by the further thought that even secular states, with no hint of religious or ethnic discriminations, are not squeaky clean. Secular states discriminate against people external to them. They also discriminate (unjustly?) between their own citizens: typically, the poor suffer radically greater restrictions than the wealthy.

I return to your ungrounded optimism, Dan, that when there exists Arab/Israeli peace, Israel could grant full rights to all. If it did, it would cease to be a Jewish state, save in name. If it did, because of Arabic population growth, it would probably cease to be a Jewish state even in name. I assume that today's Jewish Israel would oppose such consequences; in July 2018, the controversial 'nation state' law was passed, whereby Jews have a unique right to national self-determination. Jewish Israel would thus continue to find ways to discriminate for as long as it wants to remain Jewish. No doubt, Israel would be much condemned for tarnishing a liberal democracy ideal, as it has tarnished, according to many distinguished Jews elsewhere, with its 2018 *The Basic Law* that gives the Israeli Jewish people "exclusive right to national self-determination"; but condemners need reminding that their states also tarnish that ideal, if ideal it be.

I am sorry, Dan, but liberal democracy is at best an ideal that hovers in the heavens. It is an ideal that is as impossible to achieve on Earth as it is impossible for a *Jewish* state to be secular – and for human beings to be angels, however angelic the smiles. And would we want to be angels?

Mullings

Dan asks:
   Given the threats Israel faces from its Arab citizens, should their rights be curtailed?

Peter asks:
   Can a liberal democratic state exist without any unjust discriminations?

Chapter Seventeen

'Scratch an anti-Zionist and you'll find an antisemite.' Really?

17.1 DAN reflects:

Several years ago, Dawoud El-Alami – my Muslim co-author mentioned previously – and I spoke to a Christian group about the Palestine-Israeli conflict. My role was to present the Zionist case in favour of the creation of a Jewish state. I tried my best to present a reasoned argument, but a number in the audience were adamant that Jews had stolen the land from the indigenous Arab population and were vociferous in their condemnation of Israel. Later in the day a number of young actors presented an extremely bitter play castigating Israel. Dawoud and I were disturbed by the diatribes we heard. We ourselves had attempted to present a balanced approach to the subject. But it was clear that the vast majority were adamant critics of Israeli policy.

I couldn't help but wonder if lying behind such anti-Zionism was a degree of anti-Jewish hostility. No longer is it permissible to express antisemitic opinions. But, arguably, such antipathy for Israel has now become an acceptable means of expressing anti-Jewish feelings. Certainly, this is the opinion of a number of Jewish observers. In this regard the historian Robert Wistrich has argued that since 1967, antisemitism has rented leftist discourse in Britain not only through its obsessive focus on the sins of Israel, but its ideological singling out of Jews, Judaism and Zionism as dire impediments to revolutionary progress.

Certainly not all forms of anti-Zionism conform to such a pattern. Arguably, antisemitism and anti-Zionism should be sharply distinguished from one another. There are certainly critics (non-Jewish and Jewish) who are disturbed by certain aspects of Israel's policy regarding the Palestinians without in any way harbouring antisemitic sentiments. I myself have been critical of Israel. Some of my Jewish friends have castigated me for adopting such a stance. But in making a case against the harsh treatment of Palestinians, I in no way wished to criticize Jewry as a whole.

17.2 PETER reflects:

As ever, Dan, you offer some fragmentary and useful reflections – though also, now, some irritations.

You attempted a 'balanced approach' regarding the Palestinian/Israeli conflict. Why assume that there is 'balance' here of the rights and plights of the two peoples? There exist considerable sufferings and disparagements, in various dimensions, regarding different groups and time periods. It is probably impossible to justify any 'balance'.

You refer to Robert Wistrich's claim that the 'radical' Left has become highly antisemitic. I gather that he also sees that Left as influential, radically affecting political debate. My immediate scepticism comes to the fore regarding such generalizations. After all, some Jews are radical Left; and most of the radical Left would be astonished to hear that they are antisemitic – and, for that matter, influential on governments, global corporations and capitalism's ways.

Minor irritations to one side, there is the big question of the relationship between anti-Zionism and antisemitism. Quite a few Jews, as you agree, are highly critical of Israeli policies, yet are not antisemitic. They are usually only anti-Zionist in that they seek a more moderate Israel, not its non-existence. Historically, as you told me, some Orthodox Jews – surely not antisemitic – objected to any manmade creation of Israel. We agree, therefore, that antisemitism and anti-Zionism are distinct: neither entails the other. Anti-Zionism, though, may be the 'cover' for antisemitism; so, how can we tell?

Here is one way. Criticisms of Israel which can reasonably be seen as anti-Zionist are indicative of antisemitism, it is argued, if similar criticisms are lacking of other countries with disreputable policies relevantly similar to Israel's. I doubt if that 'inconsistency in criticism' is a conclusive test for antisemitism, but it may offer some evidence. Mind you, those eager to use the antisemitic accusation on such a grounding may expose themselves to various discriminatory accusations for they often do not rage to such an extent against Islamophobia, discrimination experienced by other minority groups or, indeed, the sufferings of the disabled from social benefit cuts.

Curiously, antisemitism based on the 'inconsistency in criticism' is often charged against people on the Left who criticize Israeli policies. I say 'curiously' because it is as if the critics are unaware of the Left's heavy criticisms of Islamic countries with their poor human rights records. It also ignores British governments that support Saudi Arabia through arms' sales, while criticizing Israel via various UN resolutions; those governments typically have not been charged with antisemitism. Depressingly, typically in today's Britain, even to discuss these matters, even to note some connections between Zionists and 1930's Germany, even to wonder about the political motivations of those highlighting (alleged) antisemitism on the Left, is often taken as manifesting antisemitism.

Still, let us pop the political Left/Right divide to one side. Here, we need greater clarity regarding anti-Zionism's relationship with antisemitism. I look to you, Dan.

17.3 DAN moves on:

Over the years, I have been anxious to differentiate anti-Zionism from antisemitism, despite the fact that various people apparently have been eager to conflate them. Criticism of Israel is fundamentally different from hatred of Jews. As you point out, Jews who are critical of Israeli policy are not guilty of Jew-hatred. Rather, they are alarmed by Israel's treatment of Palestinians. However, there is no doubt – at least in the Arab world – that antisemitism and anti-Israel sentiments are often merged.

During the last fifty years, considerable antisemitic literature has been published in Muslim countries utilizing religious as well as racial motifs.

As mentioned earlier in Chapter Seven, some of this literature, such as Hitler's *Mein Kampf,* Henry Ford's *International Jew* and the *Protocols of the Elders of Zion,* have been translated into Arabic and made widely available. Other writings have exploited stereotypical images of the Jew inherited from the past. These negative depictions of Jews have been reinterpreted to express Arab antipathy towards Jewry.

Smile, please, for the Jew-hater

There's a Jew, sitting in the corner of a crowded Texas bar; he sports a large Jewish star on a chain around his neck. A big, angry-looking Texan walks in, spies the Jew and bellows, 'I hate and detest Jews. Let's have a round for everyone here except for the damned Jew.' The Jew smiles.

The Texan orders more rounds, one after another, for everyone – except the Jew, as the Texan loudly makes clear.

Finally, with the Jew still smiling, now smiling broadly, the Texan says to the bartender, 'What the hell is that damn Jew grinning about? I refuse to buy him a drink. Doesn't he realize how much I hate his Jew guts?'

The bartender replies: 'Yes, sir – but Mr. Bernstein is the owner.'

Repeatedly, the Jew is portrayed as an evil force determined to corrupt and exploit the society in which he lives. In addition, Jews are presented as forming a global conspiracy intent on dominating world affairs. Tragically, such perceptions fuel antipathy toward Israel and the Jewish community world-wide. In the minds of many Arabs, anti-Zionism and hatred of Jews are inseparable.

17.4 PETER nods – and yet:

Dan, you rightly mention how critics of Israeli policies can be wrongly deemed antisemitic. To advance on this chapter's topic, though, we need to scrutinize more determinedly the apparent mistaken conflation of antisemitism and anti-Zionism.

Antisemitism is hatred of Jews just because they are Jews. That simple idea is unnecessarily complicated by the 'working definition' of antisemitism by the International Holocaust Remembrance Alliance (IHRA) as:

> a certain perception of Jews, which may be expressed as hatred toward Jews. Rhetorical and physical manifestations of antisemitism are directed toward Jewish or non-Jewish individuals and/or their property,

toward Jewish community institutions and religious facilities.

The IHRA provides examples of antisemitism, but they do not help in clarification; indeed, they seem to imply that it is antisemitic to describe Israel as an endeavour expressly for the Jews or to believe that some Jews may be more committed to Israel than to their country of current residence. (Were I an Orthodox Jew somehow trapped in Saudi, I should certainly prefer to be living in Israel and would have more loyalty to Israel.) The examples also imply that certain beliefs about Jewish culture or history must be manifestations of antisemitism rather than genuine mistakes or matters for discussion. Clarity is required.

Clarity is required because, for instance, Harry could be antisemitic yet make an exception for his Jewish friend Hanna. Zoe may hate Abe, a Jew, not because he is Jewish but because he misled her over his romantic intentions. You see, caveats and 'case by case' considerations arise, as well as matters of degree, regarding antisemitism.

Anti-Zionism also arrives as a spectrum. Let me regiment. 'Extreme' anti-Zionism would seek the removal of all Jews from the Middle East. ('Ultra-Extreme' would seek Jews' removal from the Universe.) 'Hard' anti-Zionism, claims that modern Israel, as a Jewish state, ought not to exist. Versions of 'medium to soft' anti-Zionism are critical, in varying degrees, of Israeli policies, but accept that Jewish Israel should continue in some Jewish form.

Beware appearances

'What? I've been profiting Bernstein?'

Obviously Extreme (and Ultra-Extreme) anti-Zionism is antisemitic. Hard anti-Zionism, though, can hardly count as thereby antisemitic, given that many Orthodox Jews once strongly disapproved of a Jewish Israel instituted by man – and some still do. All the softer forms of anti-Zionism are clearly not *thereby* antisemitic, not least because those forms are held by many Jews whom there is no reason to deem 'self-hating'.

The debate must be whether (non-extreme) anti-Zionists are such because of their antisemitism. Well, look at the evidence, case by case.

Given that many Jews, albeit probably a minority, hold some version of soft anti-Zionism, that is surely evidence against insisting that typically antisemitism lurks behind anti-Zionism.

Some may argue that while anti-Zionist Jews are not antisemitic, anti-Zionist non-Jews *must* be antisemitic. Whether or not that manifests an 'anti-Gentilism' by those Jews, we should look at the reasons that non-Jews have for anti-Zionism. Unsurprisingly, there is a variety of good (not thereby conclusive) reasons – to do with the suffering of many Palestinians, how modern-day Israel arose and Israel's discriminatory policies.

Zionists, I recommend, should evaluate the reasons given for the various anti-Zionist stances, instead of trying to smother debate with the blanket of antisemitism.

17.5 DAN responds:

The distinction you make between 'hard' anti-Zionism and 'soft' anti-Zionism is intriguing. You are right that Jews who are critical of Israeli policy are not antisemites. They are critics of Israel – although I should point out that they are sometimes classified by Israel supporters as 'self-hating Jews.' I think this is an unfair characterization – it is used primarily to stifle Jewish dissent about Israel. It would certainly be useful, as you suggest, to look at each instance of anti-Zionist attitudes. But, as you no doubt recognize, this is not always possible.

I should stress, however, that within the Jewish community there are staunch supporters of Israel who insist that behind anti-Zionism is invariably the shadow of antisemitism. These spokesmen are aware that there is a distinction between antisemitism and anti-Zionism but, in their view, modern anti-Zionism is a disguise for Jew-hatred. For example, in a powerful speech at the annual *Jerusalem Post* conference in New York, World Jewish Congress President, Ronald S. Lauder, presented a clear message to those who supported boycott, divestment and sanctions against Israel that anti-Zionism and antisemitism are one and the same. In the light of the UNESCO vote that denied Jewish ties to the Temple Mount, he argued that being anti-Israel is being antisemitic, plain and simple.

I have some sympathy for Lauder's characterization of contemporary anti-Zionism. Frequently, in speaking to various groups, I have been faced with hostile critics of Israeli policy. Pro-Palestinian members of audiences are invariably fiercely critical of any justification of Zionism that I make. They rage. They rant. They disparage the world-wide Jewish community. Listening to them, I have become suspicious. I fear that, in some cases, they are unleashing fury at Jews and Judaism. In the shadow of the Holocaust, it is unacceptable to criticize Jews on racist grounds. But it has become acceptable to criticize Israel. In doing so, some of these critics have found a new forum in which to express their contempt and hatred of the Jewish people.

17.6 PETER concludes:

After all this, Dan, I feel that I must repeat my recommendation:

> Zionists should evaluate the reasons given for the various anti-Zionist stances, instead of trying to close down debate by smothering it with the blanket of antisemitism.

Often, case-by-case evaluations, as you say, are impractical, but when impractical, people ought not to leap to antisemitic interpretations as if antisemitism should be the default assumption.

Yes, some argue that anti-Zionism is but a cover for antisemitism. Others argue for an 'identity' position: anti-Zionism really is just the same as antisemitism. Then, it is not a cover; a sheet cannot cover itself. On the identity view, antisemitism and anti-Zionism can no more come apart than a triangle of the Euclidean persuasion can exist without three sides. The identity view, though, is wrong – as we agree.

There is a conceptual distinction between antisemitism and anti-Zionism (hard and soft). Hence, we enter the empirical world: as a matter of fact, are *all* instances of anti-Zionism (hard and soft) accompanied by antisemitism? The answer has to be, 'No, certainly not all'. The only reasonable stance is that *some* (maybe many) instances of anti-Zionism run along with an antisemitism and – note, this is a further claim – the anti-Zionism is deliberately used as a cover.

You cite a pro-Palestinian audience that struck you as antisemitic because of its anti-Israel outbursts. That could well be a fair assessment, given the context. What is not fair, is the predisposition – maybe possessed by Lauder – to tarnish all instances of severe criticism of Israel as antisemitic.

The reluctance by many Zionists to consider anti-Zionist arguments without deeming them antisemitic perhaps shows some unease, some embarrassment, about the Zionist position, a position that heavily discriminates in favour of Jews settling in Israel and against Palestinians. That is obviously some form of ethnic discrimination.

Now, does that reflection immediately cast me, a supporter of Israel, as antisemitic – or a self-hating Jew, albeit in appearance only? Well, we are about to turn to that curious 'self-hating' topic.

> **Mullings**
>
> Dan asks:
> Does antisemitism inevitably lurk behind anti-Zionism?
>
> Peter asks:
> Are Zionists who insist that anti-Zionism is just a cover for antisemitism covering their own unease at Israel's ethnic and religious discriminatory policies?

Chapter Eighteen
Are anti-Zionist Jews nothing but self-hating Jews?

18.1 DAN introduces:

The term 'self-hating Jew' is applied to Jews who allegedly hold antisemitic views. The notion gained widespread currency following the publication of Theodor Lessing's *Der Judische Selbsthass* (*Jewish Self-Hatred*) in 1930, in which he tried to explain the prevalence of Jewish intellectuals inciting antisemitism with their views toward Judaism. Currently, the expression is often used to discount Jews who differ in their lifestyles, interests or political positions from their critics. In particular, it refers to Jews who criticize Israeli policy.

Accounts of Jewish self-hatred often suggest that criticizing other Jews and integrating with gentile society reveals hatred of one's own Jewish origins. In various Jewish publications, such as the *Jerusalem Post*, the term 'self-hating Jew' is often ascribed to those Jews deemed antisemitic. But the widest usage of the term occurs in debates about Israel, where the accusation is used by right-wing Zionists who insist that Zionism or support for Israel is essential to Jewish identity. Jewish criticism of Israeli policy is thus considered a rejection of Jewish identity itself.

The legitimacy of the term, however, is controversial. In the view of various critics, labelling others as self-hating Jews is in fact a means of establishing the legitimacy of the accusers' interpretation of the Jewish faith. Frequently those Jews who label another Jew as self-hating are seeking to claim that their own form of Judaism is normative – the correct understanding – implying that the Judaism of the accused is flawed. The accusation 'self-hating' places the person outside the boundaries of the Jewish community as defined by accusers.

The question we need to ask is whether such an interpretation is valid. When Jews criticize Israeli policy, are they in fact self-hating? Do they seek to distance themselves from their Jewish identity or heritage? Or, are they simply seeking to offer a critique of Israeli politics as they would any political position?

18.2 PETER responds:

Here is the simple argument. If anti-Zionists are antisemites (as some propose), then anti-Zionists who are Jews are Jews who are antisemites; and that amounts to those anti-Zionist Jews being individuals who hate Jews for their Jewishness. If those individuals are aware that they are Jews, then they are self-hating Jews, unless that minimalist logical deduction is beyond them – which is highly, highly unlikely (I won't quip 'being Jews').

It is clear, though, that many Jews sincerely and deeply oppose many Israeli policies, without thereby hating Jews and hence themselves. Consider the following thought experiment:

> Goldstein is a Reform rabbi. He condemns the establishment of Israeli settlements outside Israel's pre-1967 borders. He argues that Israeli military attacks on Palestinian towns are disproportionate in their ferocity. He is highly receptive to the idea that Jerusalem's holy sites should fall under a joint Palestinian/Israeli authority.

Goldstein is deemed, by many Jews, to be an antisemitic self-hating Jew. Now, suppose that the following occurs in 2025, after Israeli elections and coalition deals.

> The Israeli government radically reduces its attacks and restrictions on the Palestinians. It withdraws from some of the controversial settlements and, via Scandinavian initiatives, enters discussions with Palestinian leaders regarding special arrangements for mutual authority over holy sites.

How should the 2025 scenario be described? Maybe a few diehards will insist that the Jewish government ministers are all self-hating Jews, but that insistence lacks plausibility. Many Jews would be worried but would wish the new policies well; they would not be self-hating Jews.

How about Goldstein? Nothing has changed 'in him'. His views are now mainstream. Those who today deem him 'self-hating' would implausibly have to claim that he himself has changed from being a self-hating Jew to a Jew who no longer self-hates. That is as implausible as saying that when a man living in New York becomes a grandfather because his daughter gives birth in Jerusalem, that grandfatherly accolade results from a change 'in him'.

My Goldstein tale is but a vivid way of suggesting that what counts as 'self-hating Jew' may, in part, be a relative matter. We may, though, ask: why do we have – why do we need – the idea of the 'self-hating Jew' at all?

18.3 DAN addresses Peter's question:

I am sure your analysis is right. Not all Jewish critics of Israeli policy are self-hating Jews. Rather they are simply Jews who are censorious of the actions of the Israeli government. Ardent pro-Zionists castigate such critics for their disloyalty and are anxious to characterize them pejoratively.

As we have noted, the accusation of Jewish self-hatred is commonly levelled in discussions of Israel and Zionism, but it has much earlier roots. In *The Jewish State*, Theodor Herzl criticized enemies of his plan to create a Jewish homeland in Palestine, calling them disguised antisemites of Jewish origin. Later, Karl Straus, an opponent of Zionism, turned the argument upside down and maintained that, like traditional antisemites, Herzl was preoccupied with Jewish difference and wanted to remove Jews from Europe.

In 1930, with the publication of Theodor Lessing's *Jewish Self-Hatred*, the term came into vogue. According to Lessing, academics opposed to Zionism were self-hating Jews. Lessing – who had previously converted to Christianity and subsequently returned to Judaism – urged Jews to repudiate assimilation and embrace their Jewish roots. In particular, he was hostile to German Jews who chose to distance themselves from Judaism. He also believed that self-hatred was a phenomenon that could be found in any minority group discriminated against by a majority.

As already noted, accusations of Jewish self-hatred are now common in contemporary debates about Israel. Jews who have challenged Israeli military operations or government policy are frequently characterized in this way. Such critics as Noam Chomsky, Michael Lerner and Tony Judt have been called self-haters. I too have faced such criticism. Following the Israeli bombing of Gaza several years ago, I wrote an article in the *Western Mail* in which I castigated the Israeli government for such an action. One of my Jewish friends telephoned me to complain. 'Shame, shame, shame!' she shrieked. Stunned into silence, I was too surprised to defend myself.

18.4 PETER muses further:

Dan, if a friend was so upset by your apparent 'self-hatred', I wonder what non-friends thought. At least you merited only three 'shame's.

You allude to psychological explanations when reflecting upon how theories of self-hatred arise. My knowledge of such theories is as poor as maybe my scepticism is great. Let us try some philosophical common-sense.

A few 'men' hate themselves for being biologically male; some queasily go to extreme lengths to rid themselves of certain lengths – and other attributes. Other men are not troubled by knowing of that teeny minority. Well, I wrote that – then

Are anti-Zionist Jews nothing but self-hating Jews? 239

I noted how some men seem threatened by 'trans' people. Let us, then, think on.

A dentist is a self-hating dentist – she hates being a dentist – yet few would see that as a threat to other dentists. A blonde female may hate being blonde, yet not hate herself; she hates her characteristics because of society's sometime image of blondes as 'bimbos'. Some Muslims may be self-hating Muslims because of recent Islamic terrorists and how non-Muslims may paint them as of that terrorist persuasion. The poor may be self-hating poor not solely because of poverty, but because of the disparagement received from the well-off.

Mr. Woody Allen

'I've frequently been accused of being a self-hating Jew; now, it's true I hate myself, but not because I'm Jewish.'

The examples remind us of different features and responses to 'self-hatred'. The dentist may change occupation – the blonde may dye her hair raven black – yet sincere Muslims may not want to, cannot even, reject their religious beliefs. Jews, however much self-hating, cannot alter their genetic inheritance. Two further thoughts spring – well, limp – to mind.

First, for 'self-hating' to be useful in explaining Jews' anti-Zionism or antisemitism, we need independent characterization, otherwise the 'self-hating' accolade is just another term for a Jew who is anti-Zionist or antisemitic. What is that independent characterization? I doubt whether there is one.

Secondly, perhaps anti-Zionist Jews are not expressing self-hatred, but 'other-hatred'. Far from hating themselves, anti-Zionists are embarrassed by – depressed by; ashamed of; angry at – Jews who, through uncritical Zionist support, bring forth condemnation of Jews *qua* Jews. It may be akin to how many Muslims are embarrassed by – depressed by; ashamed of; angry at – certain other Muslims who support the issuing of fatwahs against authors, death threats to apostates and insist that Muslim women must be fully veiled when in public.

18.5 DAN reflects:

All these distinctions help to clarify what is meant by a 'self-hating Jew'. You need to remember, though, that Jewishness is traditionally understood as unalterable. Even conversion to another religion does not make one a gentile. A Jewish apostate is a Jewish sinner. As I noted at the outset, traditional Judaism maintains that a person born of a Jewish mother is Jewish. The vast majority of Jews are Jewish by virtue of maternal descent; their Jewish identity cannot be erased.

There inevitably are persons who are Jewish by biological origin but have no desire to identify with the Jewish community. Karl Marx was such. He was fiercely critical of the Jewish community. Others also have no desire to be part of the Jewish community. A number seek to escape their Jewishness by converting to another religion. It would be fair to characterize such individuals as self-hating in that they do not wish to have any connection to the tradition into which they were born. The mistake, however, is to categorize all critics of Israel as self-hating in the same way.

Nonetheless, it is easy to see why such a categorization is made by pro-Zionists. Israel is a Jewish state, founded by Jews, and largely populated by Jews. Its political leaders are Jews. It is at the centre of Jewish life. So, when it is criticized by Jews, it is obvious to staunch defenders of the Jewish way of life that such individuals have deliberately disconnected themselves from the Jewish people. Like Marx and others, they have turned against what the Jewish people hold as most dear. Such action is treachery and betrayal.

18.6 PETER concludes and muses on:

Your comments remind me of the influential philosopher, Karl Popper. As an aside – and to link with my use of Wittgenstein in Chapter One – you can find interesting and conflicting reports of how, allegedly, Wittgenstein threatened Popper with a poker at a Moral Sciences meeting at King's, Cambridge, in the 1940s. I have seen the putative poker.

According to Popper, astrology and psychoanalysis parade as empirical theories, yet evidence against them is reinterpreted to support the theories; that is, they are not open to refutation. We, Dan – you and I – judge that the range of disparate Jews who are anti-Zionist is knock-down evidence against the theory that all anti-Zionists are antisemitic; but what is the Zionist response? 'Oh, they must be self-hating Jews – and hence antisemitic.' Zionists make it virtually true 'by definition' that anyone who seriously criticizes Israel must hate Jews. 'Self-hating', then, is no more an explanation of Jewish anti-Zionism than saying that the sleeping tablets caused him to sleep because they had sleep-inducing properties.

Regarding Marx, yes, he was Jewish, but I have no idea if he hated himself. I doubt if he, for example, held the alleged Jewish belief that the virtue of man is money; mind you, he was keen to borrow from, and not repay, his collaborator, Friedrich Engels. Marx disliked many characteristics of Jews, but he did not discriminate; he disliked many characteristics of many people.

The 'self-hating Jew' is deemed such because he possesses *some* of a variety of negative emotions towards *some* of a variety of typical Jewish characteristics. One Jew hates traditional Jewish family life and its role for women; another finds ridiculous the Jewish belief that Jews are chosen; a third argues that Jews as an ethnic group is a myth. We may find not hatred, but justified criticisms, perhaps expressed with despair or bewilderment. Sometimes, we may find no hatred of 'self', but a sadness at other Jews' obsession with their past.

No doubt, a few Jews may sincerely hate being Jewish. It certainly does not follow that they are anti-Zionist or antisemitic. A woman may hate being a woman without thereby hating other women or others' femininity. A man may hate being a father without hating fathers or disparaging fatherhood. A self-hating Jew need not be a Jew who is 'other-hating' of Jews.

It is clear that not all Jewish anti-Zionists are self-hating Jews and not all self-hating Jews are anti-Zionists. Tediously, I urge: all sweeping generalizations should be mused upon – including that one. And such a quip leads us appropriately to Jewish humour.

> **Mullings**
>
> Dan asks:
> Why would a Jew hate being Jewish?
>
> Peter asks:
> Must a Jew who hates himself for being Jewish thereby hate all other Jews for being Jewish?

Chapter Nineteen
Does Jewish humour show Jews to be unfit for a state of their own?

19.1 DAN sets the scene:

Jews are used to making jokes about themselves and, as we have sought to illustrate throughout this book, it is a central dimension of Jewish life. There is a long tradition of humour in Judaism, dating back to the Torah and the Midrash. The Bible recounts how Sarah laughed when told she would have a child, and Isaac is named for that laughter. The Talmud is replete with witty asides and repartees. During the medieval period, humour was institutionalized in various customs, perhaps most famously in Purim shpiels, comic plays based on the book of Esther. In modern times beginning with vaudeville and continuing through stand-up comedy, film and television, Jews have been known for their ability to make audiences laugh. In many cases the primary aim has been to mock Jewish stereotypes.

Given the centrality of humour in Jewish life, what significance does it have for creating a Jewish homeland? The early Zionists seemed sober and serious in their advocacy of Jewish nationhood. Works by such figures as Theodor Herzl lacked any humorous content. Instead, proponents of Jewish statehood alarmingly pointed to the tragic predicament of Jews living as a minority people. In their view, Jewish life is inevitably insecure without a homeland. Israel was thus conceived as the only remedy for Jewish suffering.

Where does Jewish humour fit into this saga? Despite the seriousness of creating a Jewish state, Jews in Israel and the diaspora have retained their sense of humour. It enlivens Jewish life. A recognition of its role in sustaining Jewry through centuries of misery can remind them of the suffering of others, in particular the desolation and devastation faced by Palestinians in the occupied territories and Gaza Strip. Jewish humour can thus serve as a link between Jewish and Palestinian hardship. The ability to laugh at one's own follies and foibles can serve as a reminder of the vulnerability of others.

19.2 PETER responds:

I blame you, Dan, for proposing this chapter's curious question. Wittgenstein reflected that serious good philosophy could be a series of jokes; but why would a sense of humour ever suggest an unfitness – or, for that matter, a fitness – to have a state?

Some states, we may quip, are 'a joke' in that they are incompetently run; I shall not mention Prime Minister May and President Trump. Some states ought to be dismantled because citizens are overwhelmingly oppressed; I readily mention North Korea's Kim Jong-un. Now, a government of jokers may be no good government at all, irrespective of their joking qualities; but there's more to Jewishness than jokes.

Maybe the Jewish sense of humour betrays a characteristic that shows Jews to be unfit for a state. Obviously, Jews can run a state, even under adverse conditions – witness Israel – but 'fitness' could be a moral fitness. Recognizable Jewish humour typically suggests that Jews see themselves as a people separate from others, needing special treatment. That can undermine ideas of equality regarding universal human rights. If that undermining is sufficient to show that Jews are unfit for statehood, then it also shows that most peoples are unfit. Most states, one way or another, discriminate against 'outsiders'. Most states are grounded in a certain distinctive 'people': in Italy, most are characteristically Italians; in Japan, Japanese; in China, Chinese – and so forth.

Maybe Jewish humour points to an unhealthy underlying psychological character, such as feeling hated by others, alienated. If – *if* – that is true, then perhaps Jews deserve a state of their own – to generate some self-esteem. Mind you, we could also argue that a state of their own only aggravates their separateness; healthier, it would be, for them to integrate with other countries' communities.

Dan, of course, you are right that Jewish humour is often grounded in Jews as 'underdog', but you are wildly optimistic in seeing that as helping Jews to recognize Palestinian plights. Are you suggesting that 'if only' the Israeli leaders told each other Jewish jokes of Jewish foibles and follies, then they would empathize with the Palestinians? That sounds like a poor joke to me, meriting a 'yeah, yeah?' meaning paradoxically, 'No'.

19.3 DAN muses:

Perhaps I am too optimistic that understanding how Jewish humour has helped Jews endure hardship can serve as a bridge between Israelis and Palestinians. Yet there is no doubt that some Jewish jokes gently mock both Jews and Arabs. Here is an example:

> Following Israel's victory in the Six-Day War, a class of students is undergoing instruction in a Russian War College in the then USSR. They are discussing how a war with China might be fought with an army of only two hundred million, while the Chinese army would come close to a billion. The brightest student asks the Soviet general in charge how they could possibly hope to win against so many Chinese. The general quickly points out that Israel had just won a war with only two or three million soldiers, while their Arab adversaries had some hundred million. The student quickly responds: 'Okay. But how are we going to get three million Jews?'

The point of mentioning such jokes is to illustrate that Jews are capable of gently satirizing themselves and others. This is far removed from the seriousness of confrontation and violence. Jokes are much better than tanks and bombs. Palestinians too use humour to cope with their predicament. I have heard that Palestinian humour corresponds with Jewish humour.

Jewish and Palestinian humour is important. It is the human face of two peoples in a tortured and tumultuous conflict. Perhaps you are right that Jews will not be able to see a reflection of their own suffering in the deprivations of the Palestinian people. But the fact that Jews and Arabs are able to look beyond the violence that has erupted between them is a sign of hope for the future.

19.4 PETER muses further:

Let me return you, digressive Dan, to the topic of humour and statehood. I still struggle to grasp the relationship.

Jewish humour often has Jews belittling Jews. Maybe if a people see themselves as so downtrodden, then downtrodden they are or ought to be: only the strong deserve the statehood prize. Of course, that is a crazy argument. In any case, even with their Jewish self-disparagement, Jews clearly have had the strength to survive and re-form a nation state.

Wisdom of the duck

'He may look like an idiot and quack like an idiot... but don't let that fool you. He really is an idiot.'

How about the Jews' moral fitness for a state? Although ethics is often said to be solely about people's treatment of others – at heart, it is an urge for altruism – rightly understood it also includes how we treat ourselves, which characteristics to develop, how to comport ourselves. While individuals, and a people, ought to develop virtues and principles of honesty, compassion and courage, I place on the table for consideration the possession of a sense of humour: in particular, one that deflates tendencies towards pride, smugness and self-satisfaction. Jewish humour often manifests that deflationary disposition.

Self-deprecation can be virtuous and can be seen as a boomerang version of *schadenfreude*, that enjoyment in another's misfortunes, for which, it has been quipped, only the Germans have a special term. *Schadenfreude* and self-deprecation, I suggest, bind us as human beings.

Statehood apart, let us actively value the Jewish sense of humour. I offer it as manifesting a principle of solidarity for facing the human condition, though, to use the great Marx (Groucho): 'Don't worry; I am a man of principle – so if you dislike that one, I have plenty of others'.

19.5 DAN responds:

You are right that having a sense of humour is a vital element to a healthy approach to life. Yet, there is a side to Jewish humour which is troubling, and directly related to statehood. In *The Jewish State,* Theodor Herzl argues that Jews will never be secure in countries where they are in the minority. Jews, as a minority, are inevitably insecure and subject to victimization – hence, the need for a state of their own.

Jewish humour reinforces this perception. Repeatedly, they are portrayed as vulnerable and targets for hostility:

> A Berlin Jew is reading *Der Sturmer*, the hateful Nazi newspaper. A friend and fellow Jew asks, 'Why ever are you reading that odious propaganda?' The Berlin Jew answers, 'I read the regular Jewish newspapers about pogroms, assimilation, riots in Palestine, and then I read *Der Sturmer* about how we Jews control politics and are taking over the world. It makes me feel much better.'

There are also, though, numerous jokes which, instead of reinforcing the theme of Jewish vulnerability in a hostile gentile world, emphasize Jewish superiority:

> A Japanese, Chinese and Jewish samurai all apply for a job as chief samurai to the Japanese emperor. The Japanese samurai steps forward, opens a tiny box, and releases a fly. He draws his samurai sword and SWISH, he neatly divides the fly into two.
>
> 'What skill,' exclaims the emperor.
>
> Next, the Chinese samurai steps forward, opens a tiny box, releases a fly, draws his samurai sword, and SWISH SWISH, the fly falls to the floor neatly quartered.
>
> 'That is very, very skillful!' shouts the emperor.
>
> Then comes the Jewish samurai, who also opens a tiny box, releases a fly, draws his samurai sword, and SWOOSH, brings forth a huge gust of wind that blows through the room. But the fly continues to fly. The emperor says, 'Where is your skill? The fly isn't even dead.'
>
> 'Dead?' replies the Jewish samurai. 'Dead is easy. Circumcision–now, that takes skill!'

Jewish jokes stress the distinctiveness and otherness of Jews. Such humour underscores the Jewish determination to have a state of their own. Such jokes reinforce the Zionist assumptions about the un-assimilability of the Jewish people. Arguably, such attitudes hinder dealing rationally with Arabs living within and around Israel. In other words, a range of Jewish jokes reinforce Jewish paranoia.

19.6 PETER muses on:

We agree that Jewish humour in whichever direction – towards superiority or inferiority – emphasizes the distinctive separateness of the Jewish people. It can have unhappy outcomes regarding discrimination: 'we' are so different; 'we' need special treatment.

Jewish humour is not, of course, the cause of that distinctiveness, but the result. Other groups often emphasize their separateness, with or without humour. Many Muslims take themselves to be very, very different from those religiously impure beings, the non-Muslims; the French typically see themselves as more discerning in cuisine and romance than the British; and most Americans feel that they are far more go-getting than typical Greeks.

Some nationalities, it is said, lack a sense of humour. A friend received a distinguished prize, a few years ago, from a prestigious German association. In his acceptance speech, to a hall packed with English-speaking Germans, he started, 'In honouring me with this prize, no one can now say that the Germans lack a sense of humour'. He was met with a silence, a silence of unawareness of anything funny having been said.

Nationalities – ethnic groups, communities – differ. I should regret the passing of those differences, even though they challenge urgings for extensive non-discriminations. The challenge is not unique to Jewish identity. The United States, European nations – and many more – ever vocal in opposing unjust discrimination, discriminate. As I noted earlier, they discriminate against foreigners, 'outsiders'. Laws of the West often favour the wealthy at the expense of the poor: wealth determines where you are free to walk.

The alternative to statehood for the Jews could be assimilation, where, it is often believed, a group's distinctive characteristics are lost. If assimilation must be like that, then I should regret it – just as I regret powerful corporations and governments promoting the assimilation of different cultures into one global homogeneous economy, through, for example, a Starbucks and McDonalds in virtually every town, guided by

Google, Apple and Microsoft. Again, though, matters of degree arise: a group may be absorbed by a larger group in some respects, but not in other respects; they may preserve what is most distinctive and important to them.

Jewish humour manifests a living sense of the Jewish distinctive identity. If any group merits statehood, then the Jews do. Having said that, Jewish Israel brings with it discriminations and injustices; but are they any different from – and any worse than – those that arise through parents giving priority to their children over other children? A life, a nation, without preferences, discriminations and attachments would be a life, a nation, without substance. Mind you, has the Israeli substance, in fact, been of much good for the Jews?

Mullings

Dan asks:
 Do Jewish jokes help or hinder relationships between Israelis and Palestinians?

Peter asks:
 Is not Jewish humour valuable in reminding us that a virtuous life requires a wry self-mocking smile at our absurdities?

Chapter Twenty
What has Israel done for the Jews?

20.1 DAN sets the scene:

In ancient times the Jewish people had a country of their own. In the late nineteenth century, secular Zionists pressed for the return of Jewry to its ancient homeland. Eschewing belief in messianic redemption, they argued that this must be accomplished through the efforts of Jewish pioneers. Such figures as Theodor Herzl maintained that Jews will never be secure as long as they are a minority people living in foreign lands. Only once Jews settle in Palestine will they be able to escape from Judeophobia and persecution. According to Herzl, the building of a Jewish homeland would transform Jewish life.

Astonishingly this goal has been achieved. In just over one hundred years, Israel has become a reality, but it has not solved the problem of antisemitism. In the wake of the creation of Israel,

Arab hostility to Jewry has intensified. The Arab world is united in condemnation of the Jewish state and, in a series of wars, has attempted to drive the Jewish people into the sea. Yet, despite this bloody history, Israel has survived, and today it is a significant nuclear power in the Middle East.

In Israel and abroad, the Jewish nation is at the forefront of Jewish life. Across the Jewish religious spectrum, there is universal support for Israel, even amongst those who are vociferous critics of the current government's policy. Today, young Jews are sent to Israel to learn more about the country. Modern Hebrew is taught in religious schools. The history of the country forms an essential feature of Jewish education. News about Israeli politics is avidly read. Fundraising for Israel is a critical aspect of Jewish life.

The State of Israel has thus transformed modern Judaism. Jews throughout the diaspora look to Israel as fundamental to Jewish survival. In the shadow of the Holocaust, Jewry is determined to endure: the survival of the Jewish people and the Jewish heritage is rooted in the soil of the Holy Land.

20.2 PETER responds:

You offer a polished and positive image of Israel, as saviour, so to speak, of Jewry. The rendition for that is, I suppose, the following:

> A few Jews were determinedly committed to the re-creation of Israel; they gained support through Britain's 1917 Balfour Declaration in favour of a national home for the Jewish people; support accelerated and strengthened as a result of the Holocaust horrors. The resultant homeland, Israel, these days, receives accolades from a vast majority of Jews both within and outside that homeland. True, there are a few Jews, both within and outside, who are highly critical of particular Israeli policies. Even of those, probably a large majority still uphold Israel as a shining star, essential for the continuation of Jews, Judaism and the Jewish way of life. Only a tiny minority would call for it to lose its Jewish identity.

Yes, the Jews have much to thank Israel for – or, more accurately, they have much to thank earlier Jews for, in re-creating and sustaining Israel. We should add, as you have in other works, Dan, that today's Jews have much to thank (past and present) antisemites for – particularly the Nazis with their horrendous concentration camps and extermination aims. Without those, probably there would not have been so much Jewish determination for a Jewish Israel and so much international support by major powers; the Balfour

Declaration, those decades earlier, may have been forgotten.

In view of those points, ought we not all to feel uneasy and queasy? Should we judge that the sufferings of many, many Jews over the centuries through antisemitism, climaxing with the utter horrors, appalling pains, degradations and deaths during the Holocaust, were worthwhile – so worthwhile because they ultimately led to the Jewish Israel of today? Would it not have been better to have had no Holocaust, no antisemitism – and hence no Israel – even if it had led to Jews becoming so assimilated that very few retained a Jewish way of life?

Let me transform the question into an exclamation:

> What outrageous horrors millions of Jews have suffered for the sake of Israel!

20.3 DAN muses:

You are right about antisemitism: there is a paradox. It is a cancer in the body of society that must be eradicated. The Jewish community is united in its determination to overcome Jew-hatred whatever its form. Yet, paradoxically, at the same time, Jew-hatred has frequently led to the enrichment of the Jewish heritage. Discrimination and persecution intensified the Jewish determination to rely on God and live in accordance with the covenant.

> **'It's how you tell them'**
>
> An Israeli is visiting London Zoo, when he sees a little girl pushing her arm into the lion's cage. The lion grabs her, trying to yank her inside. The parents scream. The Israeli punches the lion on the nose. The lion lets go of the girl, jumping back.
>
> A reporter has been watching, 'Sir, that was the bravest thing I've ever seen.'
>
> 'Why, it was nothing, really,' replied the Israeli. 'The lion was behind bars. I saw a girl in danger and acted as I felt right.'
>
> The reporter remained impressed, saying that he was a journalist and the Israeli's courage and kindness would be the lead story. He took a photograph and asked for details.
>
> 'Well, I'm from Israel. I serve in the Israeli army and I vote for the Likud.'
>
> The following morning, excited, the Israeli buys the paper. There he reads on the front page, above his photograph:
>
> RIGHT-WING ISRAELI ASSAULTS AFRICAN IMMIGRANT AND STEALS HIS LUNCH

Rather than being our most ferocious enemy, antisemitism has often fostered Jewish survival. Hostility towards Judaism and the Jewish people has isolated us as a nation and intensified our determination to survive. The more the outside world detested us, the more we relied on God to save us. In the face of violence, we sacrificed ourselves to sanctify his name. Through over three millennia, we have seen ourselves as God's suffering servants. Our mission has been to serve God and advance his kingdom. We have been God's chosen people, whose destiny is to witness to his eternal truth.

Antisemitism is an evil, but it is a misapprehension to believe that the persistence of Jew-hatred has only had a negative impact on Jewish life. On the contrary, what modern Jews often fail to grasp are the positive benefits of anti-Jewish hostility. Contempt for the Jew has united the Jewish people and forced them to turn inwards. Through centuries of persecution and massacre, Jews have remained faithful to their ancient tradition. The paradox of Jewish life is that hatred and Jewish survival have been interrelated for thousands of years, and in modern times hatred of the Jew has been the underlying cause of the determination of Jewry to create a country of its own.

20.4 PETER muses in return:

There is nothing mysterious about a people holding as one when under external attack. Wars can bring people together; natural disasters generate community spirit; and government policies may produce solidarity amongst those adversely affected – witness how readily the farming community, tractors included, can organize protests in France. What is distinctive about the continual attacks on the Jews, cumulating with the Holocaust, is their giving rise to modern-day Israel, with an Arab territory swallowed by Jewry – courtesy of Jewish determination combined with guilt and unease of some major powers at the mistreatments of the Jewish people.

Dan, you speak of the Jewish community's determination to overcome Jew-hatred; but does Israel's existence help? Israel provides comfort to many Jews – knowing that there is a 'home' – but it has intensified the hatred of Jews by many Arabs. It has probably aggravated the West's antisemitism, with antisemites seeing Jews as powerful manipulators lurking behind Western politics and wealth. Of course, those antisemites, I stress again, ignore the many, many Jews who are poor, struggling for a living, both within and without Israel.

There are, then, three big questions that cast doubt on Israel's value. First, does Israel's existence help to reduce antisemitism? Secondly, does the displacement of the Palestinians sit well with how Jews would like the world to understand Jewish values? Thirdly – as already highlighted, but you danced away from it, Dan – today's Israel has resulted from centuries of vast sufferings, culminating in the Nazi's Endlösung (Final Solution): has clinging to the Jewish identity been worth all that suffering?

20.5 DAN responds:

You pose three questions. First, does Israel's existence help to reduce antisemitic attitudes? Regrettably the answer is no. Zionists were misguided in their initial optimism. That does not mean, however, that Israel should never have become a reality. For Jews, what is important is that they have a place of refuge. After centuries of insecurity, Israel provides a safe-haven from discrimination, persecution and murder.

Secondly, does the displacement of the Palestinians sit well with how Jews would like the world to perceive their Jewish values? Critics of Israel frequently point out that Israeli policy is callous and inhumane, illustrating the bankruptcy of the Jewish heritage. Yet, such criticism ignores the fact that within the Jewish community there are many who sympathize with the plight of the Palestinians. Jewry is not monolithic. Many of us are determined that just as Jews have gained statehood, so too should Palestinians.

Thirdly, you ask whether clinging to Jewish identity has been worth the suffering of the past. For Jews, that is a curious question. Across the religious spectrum, the answer would be a resolute 'Yes'. Through our history, we have regarded ourselves as God's suffering servant. This is key to Jewish theology. In the Hebrew Bible, Isaiah 53 ascribes the suffering servant to the nation of Israel who silently endured unimaginable suffering at the hands of its gentile oppressors. According to rabbinic Judaism, the final and complete redemption of the Jewish nation, which has suffered through the centuries, will stun Israel's neighbours.

Of course, many Jews do not embrace the theology outlined above. Yet, all we Jews believe that the Jewish people must endure, and that the Jewish religious tradition survive. Nothing must be allowed to defeat us. In this we are resolutely united despite the religious divisions that exist in the community.

20.6 PETER ultimately challenges:

We agree, it seems, Dan, that Israel has not reduced antisemitism's extent. While it provides 'home' for Jews, living there or not, I doubt its safety, bearing in mind Arab hostility and local population changes. As for Israel's Jewish values – well, maybe those keen on strong nationalisms are impressed, but Israel, currently, is not a great advertisement for justice, understanding, compassion and related ideals.

My biggest worry over your position, Dan, concerns how much suffering it is worth undergoing to maintain Israel. Try this. Suppose millions of Jews, including you, were offered the following deal.

One option is for those millions of Jews and their children – for you, Dan, family and Jewish friends – to undergo horrendous sufferings, starvation, medical experimentation and eventual agonizing deaths. Perhaps around six million Jews encounter those horrors in concentration camps. We label that the 'Holocaust Option'. As a result, though, modern-day Israel is created, a Jewish 'home', albeit with its insecurities and with sufferings of a large number of displaced Palestinians. That Israeli state survives at least – say – for two hundred years. Who knows what then...

The other option is: there is no Holocaust, no Nazis in power; there is no Jewish Israel. Instead, Jews preserve their way of life, their identity, in small groups spread throughout various countries. In some countries, their lives run very well; in others, they feel oppressed by antisemitism. Overall, though, things gradually improve as more countries become more secular to some degree, respecting human rights, the rights to religious expression, cultural traditions *et al*. Ideally, on that basis, there could be a genuinely secular Israel – the 'one-state' solution to the Palestinian/Israeli conflict – where different ethnic and religious groups, Jews, Muslims, Christians, Palestinians, have their different cultures respected. Of course, that solution requires welcoming arms by, and trust between, the different communities; thus, I wrote 'ideally' rather than 'realistically'.

My impression is that you, Dan, think that the vast majority of Jews, including yourself, would accept, or at least *ought* to accept, Option One, the Holocaust Option. Are you right about the 'ought'? Is the Jewish Israeli state that important? Surely, you could only think it so, if you sincerely believed it is God's will for Jews to create and maintain a Jewish state at *whatever costs*.

Our dispute comes down to your thinking you know what is best for the Jews – a Jewish Israel is best – and my knowing that I do not know. As said before, I approve of diversity; so, if we are to continue to have nation states, be they ethnic or religiously grounded, then I run with the Jewish State of Israel. Whether that Israel, in the long run, is good for the Jews, I have no idea. Whether that Israel is good for the world – well, we are about to judge.

Mullings

Dan asks:
Did Jews need a state of their own?

Peter asks:
Is the eventual existence of a Jewish Israel worth any amount of suffering by the Jews?

Chapter Twenty-One
What has Israel done for the world?

21.1 DAN sets the scene:

Throughout this book we have been debating the ways in which the creation of a Jewish state has been of benefit to the Jewish community. But has Israel contributed to the world? One of the early Zionists, Ahad Ha-Am, addressed this question. Zionism, he believed, would not solve the problem of antisemitism, but it could provide a basis for Jewish living in the modern world. Israel is to be a state infused with Jewish values, and not simply a homeland for the Jewish people.

Ahad Ha-Am was correct in believing that Israel would become the centre of Jewish life. Jews now look to the Holy Land as their cultural and religious centre. However, Ahad Ha-Am's conception of the Jewish state as representing the highest ideals of Judaism has not materialized. Besieged by enemies, Israel has been compelled to focus on military might to defend itself. What is of crucial importance is survival, and, as a result, the Jewish homeland has not realized Ahad Ha-Am's idealization of Judaism's spiritual, religious and cultural dimensions.

Critics of Israel continually point to Israel's treatment of the Palestinians in Gaza and the Occupied Territories as evidence that the Jewish people have failed to carry out the highest ideals of Judaism. You yourself, Peter, have made similar claims. Yet, it must be remembered that from the early decades of the nineteenth century, Zionists were continually under siege by their Arab neighbours. Regarded as usurpers of the Holy Land, they have been threatened with annihilation. It is not surprising that there has been little scope for Israel to shine as a beacon of light in a hostile world.

21.2 PETER responds:

Dan, you are right that I and others often point to Israel's aggressive mistreatment of the Palestinians; mind you, so have you. That suggests that at least some Jews recognize that Israel, even in adversity, could behave better.

What Israel has done for the world – well, one thing – is to manifest how a country can get away with disproportionate actions against an enemy, leading to considerable suffering. The United States has usually supported Israel in such actions. Many countries act in disproportionate ways, adversely affecting others, both within and without their borders; some engage manifestly in considerably worse actions than Israel – witness various Middle Eastern countries, Russia, and the United States' recent actions in the Middle East and past actions in Vietnam.

What Israel *ought* to have done for the world – Ahad Ha-Am, you and others suggest – is provide the world with the spiritual light of Judaic values. Despite my atheism and humanism, I could paradoxically perhaps welcome such an Israel; it could harmonize with my oft-made preference for diversity.

Any state religiously grounded – and hence Ha-Am's ideal Jewish Israel – is discriminatory, as I boringly repeat. Such states favour certain religious principles, peoples and institutions, over others. Anyone who seriously believes in utter equality regarding universal rights will find the ideal Israel offensive. As argued earlier, though, even liberal secular democracies typically offend some equalities: for example, only foreigners with certain skills or money may be permitted residence. Discriminations, of course, come in varying types and degrees. My enthusiasm for Ha-Am's Israel of Judaic values waxes and wanes, depending on how those Judaic values, in application, affect non-Jews and, for that matter, atheistic Jews.

For you, Dan, the value that takes highest priority is *survival* – survival of the Jews. My guess is that you are not so concerned about the permanent survival of other nations or ethnic groups or cultures such as those to do with Peruvians, Palestinians and Polish. I wonder why there is that discrimination, if it is indeed so, in favour of Jews.

In the previous chapter, you were prepared to accept Holocaust horrors, it seemed, if the only way for the Jewish people to survive and/or Jewish Israel to come into existence. Now, I lack conviction that survival always takes highest priority – be it survival of the Jews, the Muslims, the French; trapeze artists, Morris Dancers, the Dodo – or of me. I cannot see how anyone can be so certain that a nation, an ethnic grouping, a species, ought to survive *whatever* the costs to others.

Presidents of nuclear powers claim a readiness to order nuclear attacks. To kill millions of innocent people and non-human animals, and to destroy much of the environment to save one's own nation, are acts which strike many people as obviously the right thing to do. To my mind, it is obvious – obviously wrong, full stop. Dan, you clearly do not believe that anything, just anything, however bad for others, is justified to save the life of one individual; so, why believe it so of Jewry? My thought is that sometimes:

> Let justice be upheld, though a people perishes.

One thing that Israel has done for the world is, regrettably, to encourage nations not to believe that – but to believe in survival, whatever the costs.

21.3 DAN debates further:

I think we are at a crossroads at the end of these lengthy discussions. You are outside the Jewish community, and hence do not fully grasp the significance of Jewish survival. Across the religious spectrum – from the strictly Orthodox to the most assimilated – Jewry is united in its conviction that survival of the Jewish people and of the Jewish heritage is fundamental. It is non-negotiable. We Jews have endured for nearly forty centuries and are determined to continue. No longer are there Sumerians, Assyrians, Egyptians, or Romans. The nations that besieged us in ancient times have vanished, but we Jews have continued to exist despite repeated attempts to overwhelm and crush us. It is miraculous. In the eyes of religious Jews, it is our destiny to bear witness to the truths of Judaism as God's suffering servant.

Take ten?

God first went to the Egyptians and asked them if they would like a commandment. 'What's a commandment?' they asked.

'Well, one of them goes: *Thou shalt not commit adultery*,' replied God.

The Egyptians thought about it and then said, 'No way, that would ruin our weekends.'

So, God then went to the Assyrians and asked them if they would like a commandment. They also asked, 'What's a commandment?'

'Well,' said God, 'One says: *Thou shalt not steal.*'

The Assyrians immediately replied, 'No way. That would ruin our economy.'

Finally, God went to the Jews and asked them if they wanted a commandment. 'How much?' they asked.

'They're free,' replied God.

'Great!' said the Jews, 'We'll take ten.'

Transcending the differences that separate us, the Jewish community is determined not to grant Hitler a posthumous victory. Israel is a symbol of this determination. You are unsympathetic. You seek instead to champion universal moral ideals. You cannot see how we Jews can view history in the way we do. This is, I believe, a failure of insight. You are outside the Jewish circle and cannot see things as we do. And as a result, you do not understand why we Jews are so committed to the Jewish state. Israel cannot simply be a secular nation. The point of Israel is to provide a safe-haven for the Jewish people. It is a democracy. It upholds the rights of all its citizens, Jews and non-Jews. But ultimately it must be a Jewish homeland, a country where Jews are protected from those who hate us and seek our destruction.

21.4 PETER responds:

You speak with passion, Dan – even fury. You tell me that Jews believe themselves different and special. It is ironic that a recent Jewish report (by Staetsky) seemed to identify such beliefs as antisemitic.

I am, though, hurt, Dan. I have explicitly argued that Jewish Israel has as much right to exist as other states – for virtually all states engage in discriminations. I added my liking for diversity and hence for Israel. My caveat was that some discriminations merit greater challenge than others; my love of diversity, for example, is no *carte blanche* for the oppressive Iranian regime or for Israel's current policies that hurt the Palestinians so badly – or for its extensions of settlements beyond previously agreed borders.

You are right that I lack Jewish insight into Jewish identity, but I am not denying that such Jewish identity exists. I am denying that any nation's identity merits preserving, regardless of how tragic the consequences for others. The world has lost various nations, civilizations and ethnic groups – the Mycenaean, Nabateans and Anasazi – and has witnessed assimilations, producing, for example, mish-mashes such as the people of today's Great Britain. Would you argue that those groupings should have done anything, just anything, to have survived?

Dan, you seem to think that because Jews have survived for so long, against all odds, Jewish Israel *deserves* to continue, whatever the costs. That, though, does not follow. Antisemitism has survived throughout centuries, yet deserves not at all to continue. Survival does not establish what is right to continue. We need to assess which characteristics are in play.

Good will to all...

'Now, what can we do for the world?'

Many, many Jews characteristically value fairness, compassion and liberty, but people do not have to be Jews to uphold those values. Many Jews probably believe that, in some way, they are the 'chosen people'. That belief is uniquely Jewish, but valuing its maintenance *come what may*? Well, it depends on what may come.

I own up: you disappoint me, Dan, in linking me to the rhetoric of a 'posthumous victory for Hitler'. There is a vast difference between a Nazi programme to exterminate all Jews and my questioning whether it would be a special disaster – truly, a catastrophe – if Jews yet to be born, generations ahead, are careless about their Jewish heritage, save as some interesting history, if even that. I should bemoan the loss of the culture of the Jews, be it through future Jewish generations losing interest in their Jewishness or through Jewish infertility. Similarly, I should bemoan the loss of the cultures of the French, the Swedes and the Indians, for example.

As for my championing universal moral ideals, you sound critical; but, yes, I strongly believe, for example, that innocent people ought not to be tortured against their will for sheer fun – wherever they live. I suspect you hold to that universal ideal. I am highly critical of God, if he really did tease Abraham into a readiness to sacrifice his son. Such sacrifices I hope – be they of sons, daughters or sheep – are now off the Judaic agenda.

21.5 DAN responds:

You are right to point out that through the centuries Jews have regarded themselves as God's chosen people. This is a central theme in the Hebrew Bible and rabbinic sources. Such a conviction, though, has generally lost its hold on Jewish consciousness. Reform Judaism, for example, has reinterpreted this concept as meaning not that God chose the Jews as his special people, but that the Jewish nation chose to believe in God. We are 'the choosing people,' not those who have been divinely chosen.

Today the Jewish community does not regard itself as in any sense superior to others. But we do think we are unique. We regard our heritage (even if we do not accept its religious assumptions) as supremely valuable. The Bible, rabbinic texts such as the Mishnah and the Talmud, customs and observances – all are invaluable. We see ourselves as possessing a rich, invaluable cultural heritage. We are proud of our history, and of the esteemed Jewish figures of the past and present. We believe that we have made a major contribution to the world. But it is not because of any inherent superiority.

I think you miss the significance of our pride in the Jewish past and our determination that there should be a Jewish future. You must remember that less than a hundred years ago we were faced with annihilation. The Nazi quest to exterminate Jewry was real, and it would have eliminated us all. We Jews live in the shadow of this nightmare. It haunts us even when we feel secure. For many Jews, the creation of Israel is a living symbol of hope. It is perceived as a guarantee that we will survive no matter what enemies we might have.

This is the context for the question that we have been discussing in this chapter: does Israel have something to offer the world? In the previous chapter I argued that the creation of a Jewish state makes a profound difference to Jews. But it is difficult to see that Israel has made a contribution to others. This is largely because the Jewish state has been under constant threat. From its inception it has been under assault by the Arab world. This has hindered its capacity to incorporate the highest spiritual and ethical ideals of the tradition – ideals that include righteousness, justice and liberation from oppression.

21.6 PETER muses on:

I am impressed and slightly amused by the revision of Jews being God's 'chosen people' to being the 'choosing people', choosing God. Neither rendering holds weight for those numerous Jews lacking religious belief. 'Choosing God', of course, is no distinctive marker of religious Jews from religious non-Jews.

At heart, this chapter's question is twofold. What should we make of those 'highest spiritual and ethical values' that shine in Jewry? Might a Jewish Israel one day promote those values?

'Righteousness, justice and liberation from oppression' – those, you offer, Dan, as instances of Jewish highest values. Few non-Jews, though, declare support for oppression, injustice and wrongfulness. We need to see how Jews typically apply their highest values. We shall kindly ignore Jewish Israel's current Palestinian policies. Maybe Israel, one day, will shine the light of such values to other nations – one day – but not now, given its precarious position.

Here is the crux. Even if Israel existed in benign circumstances, even if Israel explicitly espoused those highest Jewish values, should we then welcome it as a spiritual beacon to the rest of the world? I have my doubts for three reasons already rehearsed.

First, today's Jewish values would seem essentially committed to the existence of a Jewish state and such a state discriminates in favour of Jews. If it does not, then I cannot see how it is a distinctive *Jewish* state. Hence, if – *if* – non-discrimination is shiningly important, then Israel cannot be a spiritual beacon.

Secondly, as relayed by your good self, Dan, the highest value would seem to be the existence of (as yet unborn) Jews, maintaining the Jewish traditions, in centuries ahead. Now that may well be interesting, 'nice', highly preferable even, but should that desired and desirable end justify any means, however horrendous – however unjust, oppressive and morally wrong – to secure it? Or, suppose, benignly, four or five generations on, Jewish individuals gradually lose all interest in their traditions, in their sense of Jewishness. On such a supposition, the world would have lost some variety, some diversity – sadly so, to my mind – but would it really count as an utmost, appalling disaster?

Thirdly, the commitment to 'we must survive, whatever the cost to Jews and non-Jews' is, no doubt, a tribute to Jewish determination, but also to self-interest and vanity. That commitment does not shine easily within the firmament of the highest of ethical values. It emphasizes 'us' as opposed to 'them', self-interest as opposed to other-interest. That emphasis is unlikely to be terribly helpful in promoting harmony between nations here on Earth.

Mullings

Dan asks:
  Does Judaism have a moral and spiritual contribution to make to the world?

Peter asks:
  Has modern Israel's existence served only to intensify nationalism, arrogance and self-interest?

Epilogue

DAN, in conclusion, upholds:

When Jews discuss religious matters, they generally bring to the conversation a number of assumptions. Here are some typical examples:

Distant history:

The Jewish people has survived for nearly 4000 years despite repeated attempts to annihilate Jewry.

In ancient times Jews were slaves in Egypt, but miraculously escaped from bondage.

Having conquered the Canaanites, the Jewish people established a united kingdom.

In time, the kingdom was divided into two kingdoms, one in the North and another in the South.

In the first century, Jews rebelled against Roman oppression and the Temple was destroyed and Jerusalem devastated.

Subsequent reflections:

For 2000 years, Jews lived in exile, but longed to return to their ancient homeland.

For nearly twenty centuries, Christianity oppressed Jews living in Christian lands.

At the end of the nineteenth century, secular Zionists paved the way for the creation of a Jewish state in Palestine.

The State of Israel provides a means by which Jews can escape from oppression.

The Arab world is to blame for the hostile relations between Israelis and Palestinians.

Both the Jewish people and the Jewish heritage must survive.

The aim of this book is to provide a framework for exploring these and other beliefs. Peter Cave is an outsider – he has not lived and does not live within any Jewish tradition – and brings philosophical scrutiny to bear on these convictions. Repeatedly he has asked the kind of questions non-Jews want to ask, but they are often too embarrassed to raise. If they do, they fear they will be labeled antisemitic, antisemites.

We began our discussion by exploring the nature of Jewishness, and then moved on to a wide range of issues. Throughout I have tried to explain that despite our diversity, we Jews view ourselves as one family. In numerous ways we are dysfunctional. We are highly critical of each other; we are quarrelsome. We relish disagreement. It might surprise outsiders to know that such debate is an essential aspect of Jewish life. Our religious texts (such as the Mishnah and the Talmud) as well as rabbinic commentaries on Scripture are driven by argumentative conflict.

Yet despite such confrontation, we are united in our aspirations for Jewish survival. At the end of the nineteenth century there was considerable dissension about the establishment of a Jewish state in the Holy Land. Yet, as time passed – particularly with the rise of Nazism –the overwhelming majority of Jews became ardent supporters of a Jewish homeland. Even those Jews today who are highly critical of Israeli policy are determined that Israel must endure. Some of us are keen to see the creation of a Palestinian homeland, yet in advocating Palestinian statehood, we have not abandoned our support for Israel.

At numerous points, particularly in the last chapter, Peter has questioned why Jews and Judaism need to exist. He writes:

the highest value would seem to be the existence of (as yet unborn) Jews, maintaining the Jewish traditions, in centuries ahead. Now that may well be interesting, 'nice', preferable even, but should that desired and desirable end justify any means, however horrendous – however unjust, oppressive and morally wrong – to secure it? Or, suppose, benignly, four or five generations on, Jewish individuals gradually lose all interest in their traditions, in their sense of Jewishness. On such a supposition, the world would have lost some variety, some diversity – sadly so, to my mind – but would it really count as an utmost, appalling disaster?

Right or wrong, Jews would see the disappearance of Jews and the Jewish heritage as a complete disaster. We Jews are totally committed to continued existence. This is existence for its own sake. But at the same time, we believe that we have been and can continue to be a light to the nations: the Hebrew Bible has deeply enriched humanity and has served as a foundation for Christian and Muslim theology. Peter appears not to be convinced that there are unique spiritual and moral riches within the tradition. I believe he is wrong about this. Maimonides' reflections on charity (tzedakah), for example, serve as a model of humanitarian concern, and are as relevant today as they were in the twelfth century. Judaism is not superior to other faiths, but alongside the great religions of the world, it has enriched human life.

Readers will need to ponder such issues for themselves. It is our hope that we have been able to focus on central questions related to Jewishness and the Jewish state. We have wanted to examine topics that non-Jews, as well as Jews, wish to understand. Our aim has been to stimulate reflection and encourage others to think about the questions we have asked. If we have succeeded in awakening a sense of curiosity, then we will have succeeded.

PETER's many 'last word' words:

Dan has extolled the unique spiritual and moral riches within the Jewish tradition, riches widely embraced by Jews, even those uncommitted to Judaism. Yet what are they? They are values such as kindness, charitable giving, justice, respect, freedom. They, though, are not unique to Judaism and not especially manifested in Jews over non-Jews. Even if – *even if* – Dan is right that those values were brought to the world solely by Jews, it does not follow that they would cease to be recognized, were future generations to be unbothered by Jewish customs, traditions and 'being Jewish'.

Epilogue 289

Many, many Jews have done wondrous things. Most Jews are pretty decent people, as are most non-Jews. Jewishness, though, harbours attitudes, beliefs, feelings that are troubling. Such attitudes, beliefs and feelings are not unique to Jewry. Versions exist in Christianity, Islam, Hinduism; versions exist in nationalisms, ideologies and ethnicities. We find versions in ourselves. They are manifested by a heavy underlining of the distinction between 'us' and 'them', with a strong preference for 'us' as, in some way, *preferred* and deserving of that preference.

The United States provides a nationalist example: many, probably most, US citizens believe the US to be the greatest nation on Earth; it would be a disaster, they believe, were American culture to be lost. Of course, many outside of the US disagree. A clear religious example is that of Islam. Jewry constitutes another example – of some distinction.

One distinction is Jewry's remarkable – and remarkably long – unhappy history as recipient of abuse, horrors and the appalling attempted eradication. Another distinction is how the then despair led to modern Israel's creation through territorial conquest, backed internationally, ultimately manifesting 'might is right'. It is no wonder that Jews maintain a strong sense of 'us' as opposed to 'them'.

I label the above emphasis on 'us *versus* them' a 'sickness'. Maybe it coheres with a mantra from Immanuel Kant, that great Enlightenment figure met earlier: 'out of the crooked timber of humanity, no straight thing was ever made'. Here are two examples of Jewish values, gnarls in that timber – we find similar ones of other groupings –

Dan's rabbinical rhetoric tells of the wonderful morally rich values of Jews, yet, as Dan explains, for Jews, Israel must exist as a Jewish state.

If it is to be a Jewish state, it manifests discrimination in favour of Jews over non-Jews – so much for sparkles of equal rights and justice.

Dan tells us of the Jewish values of compassion, charity, liberty, respect for human life.

The test for holding such values is living by them under adversity. Those values, though, fade away when the going gets tough for Jewish Israel – witness Israel's ferocious attacks on Gaza in May of 2018 – as they do when other nations feel vulnerable: witness the United States' Guantanamo Bay dealings. It is, for example, easy for a nation to stand by its 'non-torture' policy when in benign conditions; it is when it is under threat that we see whether it really holds torture to be beyond the moral pale.

*

Throughout our discussions, I have played the role of a Socratic gadfly, albeit a humble gadfly, stinging Dan with awkward questions.

Dan has taught me much about Jewish history, values and ethos. I have usually sought to reveal inconsistencies, moral dubiety or beliefs deserving challenge, even at the risk of causing offence. As J. S. Mill argued, free speech is essential for a flourishing society; offence in itself should not be deemed a harm. As ever, though, there are grey areas; there are times and places – 'to every thing, there is a season', to quote the narrator of Ecclesiastes. What may be rightfully discussed here would be discourteous in some arenas, even incendiary in others.

I could have performed similar gadfly stingings – also humbly so, of course – had the discussions engaged Christians and Christianity or the United States and its global policies, or we human beings and our mistreatments of non-human animals.

In all this, one value that I embrace is freedom to speak, to question, to challenge, to tell jokes, to draw pictures (even to sing – well, that depends) instead of being cowed into silence, fearing hovering spectres of charges of antisemitism or Islamophobia – or some other undesirable 'ism' or 'phobia'. My expressed questioning of secular liberal democracies, as smugly ignoring their own discriminations, and my easy-going muddling support for a Jewish Israel, despite its discriminations, will, no doubt, offend my many liberal acquaintances. Yet my emphasis that Israel is indeed obviously ethnically discriminatory, and my scepticism of the insistence that preserving Jewish identity always merits highest priority, will, no doubt, offend many Jews.

Thus, it is that, in trying to discuss matters openly and honestly – seriously, yet with humour – one may become lonely.

*

In *Beyond Good and Evil*, Friedrich Nietzsche – the nineteenth-century philosopher, mistakenly linked to the origins of the Nazis' ideal – wrote:

> Isn't living assessing, preferring, being unfair, being limited, wanting to be different?

Ideals of equality, liberty and justice glimmer in heavens, be they Judaic, Christian, Islamic, secular *et al*; but once down in the swamps and crooked timbers of the real world, those ideals shine not so brightly – not so brightly at all, for we have preferences: we discriminate in favour of some over others; we prefer the red to the blue. As ever, what matters are the matters of degree – of how extensive, how deep, how offensive are our discriminations. Here in reality's muddy muddles, I am reminded of William Blake's *The Sick Rose*:

O Rose thou art sick.
The invisible worm,
That flies in the night
In the howling storm:
Has found out thy bed
Of crimson joy:
And his dark secret love
Does thy life destroy.

Jews – Israel, Judaism – are guilty of many injustices as well as justices. There are invisible worms within their riches, but those worms are to be found in all nations, ethnicities, religions – indeed, in us all.

Let us not pretend otherwise.

Parting shots

Dan reflects:
   How odd of God to choose the Jews.

Peter quotes Wittgenstein:
   How small a thought it takes to fill a whole life.

Bibliography

Avineri, S. *The Making of Modern Zionism*. New York: Basic Books, 1981.
Avnery, Uri. "In Praise of Emotion." *Tikkun*, April 20, 2013.
Black, Ian. *Enemies and Neighbours: Arabs and Jews in Palestine and Israel, 1917–2017*. London: Allen Lane, 2017.
Cave, Peter. *The Big Think Book: Discover Philosophy Through 99 Perplexing Puzzles*. London: Oneworld, 2015.
———. *Ethics: A Beginner's Guide*. London: Oneworld, 2015.
Cohn-Sherbok, Dan. *Antisemitism: A History*. Sutton: Stroud, 2002.
———. *The Palestinian State: A Jewish Justification*. Exeter: Impress Books, 2016.
Cohn-Sherbok, Dan, and Lavinia Cohn-Sherbok. *The American Jew*. London: Harper Collins, 1994.
Ha-Am, Ahad. *Nationalism and the Jewish Ethic*. New York: Schocken Books, 1962.
Herzl, Theodor. *The Jewish State*. London: Penguin, 2010.
Horowitz, Roger. *Kosher USA: How Coke became kosher and other tales of modern food*. New York: Columbia University Press, 2016.
IHEU (International Humanist and Ethical Union). *Freedom of Thought Report*. London: IHEU, 2017.
Kant, Immanuel. "Idea for a Universal History with a Cosmopolitan Aim." In *Anthropology, History, and*

Education, translated by Mary Gregor. Cambridge: Cambridge University Press, 2007.

Locke, John. *Two Treatises on Government*. Edited by Peter Laslett. Cambridge: Cambridge University Press, 1970.

Mendes-Flohr, Paul, and Jehuda Reinhard, eds. *The Jew in the Modern World: A Documentary History*. Oxford: Oxford University Press, 1980.

Mill, John Stuart. *On Liberty and other writings*. Edited by Stefan Collini. Cambridge: Cambridge University Press, 1989.

Nietzsche, Friedrich. *Beyond Good and Evil: Prelude to a Philosophy of the Future*. Edited by Rolf-Peter Horstmann and Judith Norman. Cambridge: Cambridge University Press, 2002.

Roy, Sara. "If Israel were smart: In Gaza." London: *London Review of Books*, July 15, 2017. https://www.lrb.co.uk/v39/n12/sara-roy/if-israel-were-smart

Staetsky, L. Daniel. *Antisemitism in Contemporary Great Britain: A Study of Attitudes Towards Jews and Israel*. London: Institute for Jewish Policy Research, 2017.

Wistrich, Robert. *A Lethal Obsession: Anti-Semitism from Antiquity to Global Jihad*. New York: Random House, 2010.

Wittgenstein, Ludwig. *Culture and Value*. Translated by Peter Winch. Oxford: Blackwell, 1998.

———. *Philosophical Investigations*. Translated by G. E. M. Anscombe. Oxford: Blackwell, 1953.

Further reading

Biale, David et al. *Hasidism: A New History*. Princeton: Princeton University Press, 2018.
Chomsky, Noam, and Ilan Pappé. *On Palestine*. London: Penguin, 2015.
De Lange, Nicholas. *An Introduction to Judaism*. Cambridge: Cambridge University Press, 2010.
Dershowitz, Alan. *The Case for Israel*. Hoboken, NJ: Wiley, 2004.
Gilbert, Martin. *Israel: A History*. London: Black Swan, 1999.
Goldberg, David. *To the Promised Land: A History of Zionist Thought from Its Origins to the Modern State of Israel*. London: Penguin, 1996.
Laqueur, Walter, and B. Rubin, eds. *The Israel-Arab Reader: A Documentary History of the Middle East Conflict*. London: Penguin, 2016.
O'Brien, Conor Cruise. *The Siege: The Saga of Israel and Zionism*. London: Weidenfeld and Nicolson, 1986.
Pappé, Ilan. *Ten Myths about Israel*. London: Verso, 2017.
Schindler, Colin. *A History of Modern Israel*. Cambridge: Cambridge University Press, 2013.
Schulze, K. E. *The Arab-Israeli Conflict*. Abingdon, Oxon: Routledge, 2016.

On what not to say

The founder of Feinberg tool company goes on vacation, entrusting his company to his assistant, Harry Schwartz, and his son, Mortimer. Mortimer has just graduated from Harvard with an MBA. After several days away, Feinberg phones to see how everything is going. Schwartz says he must come home immediately. He tells Feinberg he will understand the problem as soon as he is back on the highway.

Anxiously he flies back and once on the highway approaching his home town, he sees a huge billboard with a picture of Jesus on the cross. Underneath it says:

THEY USED FEINBERG'S NAILS.

Feinberg is mortified; he had spent years working on public relations. At the factory he is furious with his son. 'How could you be so stupid!' he exclaims. The son is very sorry and says he knows what to do.

The next day a new billboard goes up. On it is the same picture of Jesus on the cross. But underneath is the caption:

THEY DIDN'T USE FEINBERG'S NAILS.

298 *Jews: Nearly Everything You Wanted to Know*

Oy vey

'So much for the MBA'

Acknowledgement

The authors would like to express their many thanks to the people of Equinox – notably to Reuben Israel, Mark Lee and Sarah Hussell – for dealing with us so kindly and efficiently. Sarah deserves extra special thanks for having suffered most from our frequent questions, worries, mind changes – and muddles. Of course, considerable appreciation also goes to Janet Joyce for taking on this project.

Index

(The topics listed are all related to Jews, Judaism or Israel.)

Abbas, Mahmoud, 138, 181, 193–94
Ahad Ha-Am, 61
Allen, Woody, 239
animal welfare, ch. 4 *passim*
antisemitism, ch. 17 *passim*
    and dietary, 44
    Arab, 60
    Holocaust, ch. 6 *passim*
    Jewish survival, 262
    spelling, *xv*
anti-Zionism, ch. 17 *passim*
apartheid, chs 14, 16 *passim*
Arab-Israeli War, 211
Arab nations, 117–20
Aristotle, 167
art analogy, 5
assimilation, 57–58, 71, 237, 255–56, 277
Avnery, Uri, 165, 167

Balfour Declaration, 64–65, 73, 115, 259–60
belief, 19–20
Ben-Gurion, David, 79

Blake, William, 292–93
boycotts, ch. 14 *passim*
Buber, Martin, 155

Camp David summit, 168, 170
circularity, 108
collective responsibility, ch. 10, *passim*

definitions, ch. 1 *passim*, 119–120, 151, 170–71
democracy, chs 6, 12, 16 *passim*, 276
dentists, self-hating, 239
diaspora, chs 8, 10
discriminations, ch. 16 *passim*, 50, 120–22, 125, 151–52, 272–73
diversity
    Jewish, 12, 286, 287
    value, 58, 81, 123, 204, 268, 277
duck/rabbit, 66

El Alami, Dawoud, 119–120, 173–74, 219

Engels, Friedrich, 243
Eretz-Israel, 111

family honour, 135–36
family resemblances, 7, 9, 13, 28
Ford, Henry, 224

Gaza, chs 9, 10, 11, *passim*
genocides, 71

Herzl, Theodor, 55, 60, 72, 73
Hitler, Adolph, 6, 52, 83, 87, 101, 11, 276, 278
Holocaust, ch. 6 *passim*, 56, 65, 259–60;
and 'Shoah', 80
Holy Land, ch.11 *passim*
Humpty Dumpty, 15

IHRA, 225
Iran, 153, 156–57, 162, 277
Islamophobia, 84, 222
Israel
    Declaration of, 79
    democracy, ch. 12, 16 *passim*
    Jewish state, ch. 15 *passim*
    populations, 151
    suffering for, 266–68
    survival as Jewish, 195–96
    The Basic Law, 218
Israel/Palestine
    conflict, *xi–xii*, chs 11, 13 *passim*

Jabotinsky, Vladimir, 119–20

Jerusalem, 145–49
Jesus, 88, 107, 136
Jews
    diaspora, chs 10, 15, 20 *passim*
    future of, 60, 273–74
    hatred of, ch. 7 *passim*
    identity, ch. 1 *passim*
    Islam difference, 93
    Israel and, ch. 20 *passim*
    self-hating, ch. 18 *passim*
    world and, ch. 21 *passim*
Jewish
    homeland, ch. 5 *passim*
    humour, ch. 19 *passim*
    morality, chs 3, 4 *passim*
    narratives, chs. 5, 13 *passim*
    self-determination, ch. 16 *passim*
    values, chs 1. 20, 21 *passim*
Jews for Justice, 124–45
Jews outside Israel, ch. 8 *passim*
Judaism, ch. 2 *passim*; Orthodox 21–22

Kant, Immanuel, 31, 167, 290
Kashrut, ch. 4 *passim*
Kierkegaard, Søren, 23
King's College, Cambridge, 27, 104

Lauder, Ronald S., 229
Law of Return, 60, 197, 199, 202
Lessing, Theodor, 237

Liberal democracy myth, ch. 16 *passim*
liberty, 123, 278, 290, 292
Locke, John, 116–17
Love, 19–20

Marx, Groucho, 252
Marx, Karl, 243,
masturbation, 29, 31
Mein Kampf, 87
Meir, Golda, 86
meaning, 5–6, 14–15,
Memory, 61–66 *passim*
Mill, J. S., 122, 291,
Moses, 33
Moynihan, Daniel, 215
muddling through, 172–74, 183
Muslims, ch. 12 *passim*

Nakba, 67, 80
Nationalities, 255
Nazis and
    kashrut, 42
    Zionism, 69
Netanyahu, Benjamin, 181
Nietzsche, Friedrich, 292
NIMBY, 71
Nordau, Max, 97

Obama, President, 142

Palestinians, chs 6, 9, 11,13 *passim*
    in Israel, ch. 16 *passim*
    protests by, 61–62, 111
    Israeli support for, 134–35
personal identity, 108–9
Popper, Karl, 242

pro-semitism, 153

religious belief, ch. 2 *passim*
    indoctrination, 26
rights, chs. 12, 16 *passim*

Saudi Arabia, 152, 156–57, 210, 222, 226
self-hating examples, 238–40
Shulhan Arukh, chs 2, 3 *passim*
South Africa, 177, 188, 206, 209, 215
State as ringmaster, 75–77
Straus, Karl, 237
survival of,
    Jews, chs 8, 15 *passim*
    whales, 80–81

territorial rights, chs 5, 9 *passim*
The Sick Rose, 293
Treaties, 62, 160

Uganda Plan, 60–61
UN resolutions, 66, 111, 115, 116, 138, 179, 207

values, detached, 108
virtues, 122, 160–63, 167

West Bank, chs 9, 10, 11 *passim*
Wistrich, Robert, 220, 221
Wittgenstein, Ludwig, 5–6, 14–15, 264, 242, 247, 293
    poker incident, 242

Zionism, chs 5, 6, 17 *passim*
    as heresy, 55
    spectrum, 226–30 *passim*

www.ingramcontent.com/pod-product-compliance
Lightning Source LLC
Chambersburg PA
CBHW071957220426
43662CB00009B/1163